WOODCRAFT

D1452921

the text of this book is printed
on 100% recycled paper

Woodcraft

by Bernard S. Mason

Illustrations by Frederic H. Kock

 BARNES & NOBLE BOOKS

A DIVISION OF HARPER & ROW, PUBLISHERS

New York, Evanston, San Francisco, London

A hardcover edition of this book is published in the United States by A. S. Barnes & Co., Inc. It is here reprinted by arrangement.

First BARNES & NOBLE BOOKS edition published 1974.

STANDARD BOOK NUMBER: 06–463379–9

This volume is Part 2 of a three-part series. Each volume may be used independently of the others, or the volumes may be used together to form a complete Woodcrafts Library. The three parts are *Camping Crafts, Woodcraft,* and *Crafts of the Woods.*

You will notice that each chapter heading contains two numbers. The large Arabic number indicates the chapter number within the volume, and the smaller Roman numeral shows the chapter number within the total series. Chapters I to VIII are in *Camping Crafts,* chapters IX to XVI are in *Woodcraft,* and chapters XVII to XXIV are in *Crafts of the Woods.*

The illustrations are numbered consecutively throughout the series. Figures 1 to 100 appear in *Camping Crafts,* figures 101 to 197 are in *Woodcraft,* and figures 198 to 294 are in *Crafts of the Woods.* Each volume contains its own index.

CONTENTS

1

CHAPTER IX

CACHES

T IS SAID of a certain missionary who lived a long life among the Indians in Minnesota, that on the day of his departure for a vacation back in the East he turned to his Indian guide and asked, "How can I lock up my cabin so that everything will be safe until I return?" The Indian looked puzzled for a moment and then asked, "Why lock it up? There isn't a white man within a hundred miles of here!"

Times have changed. The Indian of the old school was an individual of fine moral stamina and could be depended upon to be completely and consistently honest whenever and wherever one found him. So, too, with the white woodsman and halfbreed of the bush who regard the stealing of another's property in the wilds as unthinkable. In the woods such things just aren't done. I have seen snowshoes hanging in an uninhabited cabin that was open for the use and convenience of any traveler who happened along, waiting there for their owner who would return for them with the coming of winter—and they surely would be there untouched when he came. Likewise I have seen traps hung up in plain sight and left throughout the summer.

A cache of food was inviolate. For no greater crime could be conceived in the wilds than the taking of food from a cache for it might mean death by starvation to the owner who relied upon it for his return trip. Many are the instances that could be recorded of city travelers half starved in an inhospitable wilderness that refused to yield either fish or game, rushing eagerly for a cache of food which they unexpectedly came upon, only to be prevented from touching it by their guide who stated simply that it did not belong to them and they could not have it.

Such was the code of the woods. And even today, if one is far enough back in the wilds, the same code holds. But now-a-days there are renegades no end in much of the woods who are products of a different culture and who know not the unwritten laws of the wilderness.

In yesteryears the art of caching was to protect food and other articles from animals. But today the light-fingered plunderers of the woods are not only of the animal but of the human kind, which adds complications. However, the chief problem today, as always, is that of protecting from animals which are everywhere present even on the outskirts of the city. Men, if they are so inclined, can ferret out the cache and get to it as easily as can the owner when he wants it again, but the duffel can be so placed that animals, even though they will spot it more easily than men, can get to it only with great difficulty if at all.

And an additional problem sometimes arises in protecting certain types of food, such as meats and liquids, from spoiling. This necessitates the use of some sort of cooler or smoker.

DRY CACHING

It depends on how long we are going to stay, the conditions of the country, and the probable hazards. An overnight camp will necessitate certain simple safeguards. In camping on the same spot for several days the main supply of food will have to be stored more securely. And again if we are leaving food for use on the return trip, still other devices may be employed. Dry caches are used for all materials except those that are apt to decay.

Overnight Caches

Right here is where the average camper does not bother and often to his grief. Never suspecting the hundreds of wild eyes that are watching his coming and going, the hundreds of keen noses that detect his presence, the camper assumes that there are no animals in these parts and thus lets his food lie. But wherever one goes in the fields, woods, or city parks, the grass and brush are alive with creatures from field mice on up whose curiosity will lead them into everything exposed. The wise camper has long since taken on the habit of putting everything destructible out of reach, whenever and wherever he camps.

Mr. Porcupine is the worst offender—he will chew up anything and everything that has grease or salt on it, and this means everything handled frequently by human hands. Evidences of his gnawing teeth can be seen around almost every cabin and lumber camp in the woods. He will gnaw up the floorboards or any other wood to get the taste of salt or grease. Ax-handles comprise one of his favorite diets—the ax should be put in the tent with you, or under your blankets if sleeping outside. Likewise, canoe paddles are a delicacy to the porcupine, particularly the sections held in the hands—they too should be elevated or covered. Squirrels will gnaw holes in any cloth, including food packs made of heavy canvas. And field mice will do likewise. Wolverines will destroy anything and everything merely for the sake of destroying it. But while one has to be far back in the woods to encounter wolverines, bears and wolves, yet the squirrels and mice are everywhere and porcupines turn up much more frequently than one expects and in all sorts of unanticipated places.

Dogs are always a hazard to the food supply and if they are in the region all foods must be placed well out of their reach. And horses, too! Last summer while camping in an Indian village I left a food pack hanging on the top of a fence-post only to find the pack down, the contents scattered, and much of it ruined—the villains were nothing more vicious than a couple of innocently grazing horses.

All of which says emphatically that all foods and everything destructible should be hoisted every night. This is a routine policy and a regular habit of every experienced camper.

Strap the food packs and hang them up on a tree as near as possible to the tent. And if you plan to be away from the spot for any length of time, they should be hoisted higher by one of the methods discussed in the following section on "Elevated Caches."

All kettles containing food should be hung as high as you can reach on stubs of branches from a tree. If there are no natural hooks, make some by striking your ax vertically into the tree, withdrawing it, and driving a peg into the crack. The green wood will spread and the peg will enter much like a wedge, making a solid hook. When you leave the spot yank out the peg and the vertical wound will soon heal to do no damage to the tree. Such pegs are used regularly by woodsmen and campers not only for kettles, but for hats and food packs, etc.

If the article contains food, or has been in contact with grease or salt and is destructible by gnawing teeth, get it up high.

Elevated Caches

If we are to camp on the same spot for several days an elevated cache of some sort should be rigged up that will at once protect the food from everything from ants to bears. The quickest and best way to accomplish this is to erect a horizontal pole between two trees, about fifteen feet off the ground, as shown in C, Figure 101. This pole should be peeled and smoothed so as to offer a less inviting surface to squirrels and similar climbing animals. It can be easily installed by using two forked sticks by which to hoist it and shove it into the crotches of the branches high over one's head, and once there it's up to stay for a rope will yank the packs up to it and lower them when needed. Of course the food must be protected from rain, and if no waterproof pack is to be had, it should be wrapped in waterproof canvas, very tightly for protection against ants, and then hoisted. Tie a rope to the pack, throw it over the pole, pull the pack up to within a few inches of the pole, and tie the end of it to a tree as illustrated.

Held aloft in this way the packs are safe from dogs, wolves and similar animals because such animals are stymied if their prey is over their heads. But bears can climb trees, and no method of caching is one-hundred per cent secure against them—not only have they rare climbing ability and great strength, but they are most persistent and stubborn cusses with their nose focussed on food. However, the horizontal pole has proven itself to be a reasonably adequate safeguard against them provided the trees selected to support the pole are too small for them to climb conveniently and yet too large for them to shake violently enough to dislodge the pole.

Another device frequently used in connection with this horizontal-pole type of cache is to tie two sticks together in the form of a cross as illustrated in D, and to tie the food bags to the ends of the sticks of the cross. When this arrangement is pulled up within a foot or eighteen inches of the horizontal pole, it sways and swings with the wind and neither animals nor ants are apt to invade it successfully.

A simple way to cache, if one does not have a rope, is merely to shove the tip of a long sapling through the crotch of a branch as shown in A, Figure 101. To hoist such a cache, tie the food bag on the tip of the sapling before it is lifted to the tree, then shove the butt

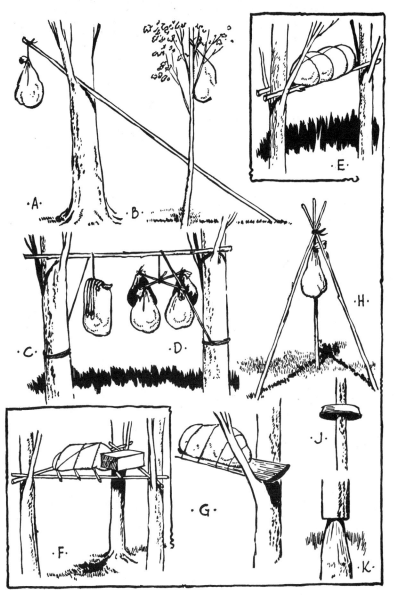

Figure 101. METHODS OF CACHING

through the crotch as far as possible, counting on its weight to drop it low enough to be reached and pulled down to the ground, thus lifting the pack. In lowering the cache merely shove the sapling up through the crotch far enough so that the weight of the food bag will drop it.

Still another device commonly used in the woods is to bend a slender sapling over, attach the food pack to it and then allow it to spring back erect again—this is shown in B. To lower a sapling, climb it until your weight tips it over far enough so that your partner can grab the end of it and attach the pack. This cache is handy for squirrels and ants, but is otherwise safe enough.

These simple methods of caching have come down to us from the Indians who found caching an everyday necessity, but there were other methods prevalent among them, particularly the use of elevated platforms. Sometimes three or four poles were attached to as many trees as illustrated in F, cross-poles placed across them, and the food securely tied on the platform thus made. Or, if the amount of food was smaller, two poles were tied one on each side of the adjoining trees as in E, thus making a narrow platform but one wide enough to hold a pack of usual size. Among the Indians of the Northwest Coast, the usual custom was to erect a slab of cedar in the crotches of branches as shown in G, on which the food was securely tied.

The tripod cache illustrated in H was common among the Indians when there were no suitable trees handy. Such a tripod was a very typical sight standing alongside the Plains Indian's tepee, displaying his shield, sometimes his headdress carrier, and hoisting the food bags out of reach of the ever eager dogs.

In their permanent villages some of the tribes of eastern Indians would build a sort of tiny log cabin hoisted on poles several feet off the ground, in which grain and other foods were stored, most of these being so tightly built that worms, ants and other insects could not enter, and the poles supporting them being fashioned in such a way that animals had difficulty climbing them. One of the devices to prevent animals from climbing a pole is shown in K—the smooth, peeled pole is whittled down to a cone shape near its top, leaving a sharp shoulder over which small animals such as squirrels and mice would have trouble in passing. A method often used by the pioneer to accomplish the same end is shown in J—a hole is cut in the bottom of a tin pan, the pole whittled down to a shoulder and the pan slipped over it.

Cupboards.—If one has a wooden packing box and plans to camp on the spot for several days, he may want to build the elevated cupboard shown in Figure 102. These are particularly handy at our favorite camping places where they remain as more or less permanent equipment, ready and waiting for us each time we come. Shelves

Figure 102. A Camp Cupboard

should be built in them and a drop front made of oilcloth. Between meals the cupboard can be hoisted up out of the reach of animals by means of the rope, and if pulled solid against the horizontal pole or branch supporting it, it will not sway in the wind as much as if allowed to hang any distance below it.

Island Caches

A policy followed by many Indian tribes living on rivers or lakes is to cache their main supply of food on tiny islands some distance out from the shore. Surrounding it by water in this way, they succeed in cutting down very materially the number of animals that can reach it. Dogs, however, have been known to swim a considerable distance to reach such caches. But separated from the shore, even by only a few feet of water, the food is much safer than on the mainland.

Caching Emergency Supplies on Trips

It is a fundamental policy for travelers in the woods to cache enough supplies along the way to guarantee beyond the slightest shadow of a doubt that adequate food will be had for the return trip. The records of exploration and even of canoe trips for pleasure are filled with pathetic tales of the tragic end of parties that failed to cache along the way, optimistically relying on the game and fish that they would catch. Without the insurance of ample caches, no one should venture beyond the range of the trading posts. It is obvious that as much food will be required coming out as going in, and common sense dictates that this should be cached and not hauled all the way in and then out again.

The common method of making caches of this type in years past has been to place the food on a layer of rocks or logs and then to cover it with a large number of rocks as heavy as can be lifted. No effort was made to conceal the cache since caches were regarded as sacred in the woods and one could be sure that it would not be mo-

Figure 103. CROSS-SECTION OF A PLAINS INDIAN UNDER-GROUND CACHE

lested by human hands. There were two dangers—dampness leading to mildew, and animals. If the provisions were carefully packed in the waterproof food-bags used by wilderness campers and placed on a slight elevation of rocks or logs, the danger from dampness and mildew is minimized. And covered with heavy rocks, the food is reasonably safe from all animals except bears. Now-a-days when precautions must be taken against human hands as well as animals, it is sometimes necessary to conceal the food and this can usually be done by placing it in hollow logs or hiding it underneath fallen logs, covering it well with rocks, and then camouflaging the whole cache with brush and other debris.

It was in underground pits that the Plains Indians concealed their pemmican or dried buffalo meat, caching it after the buffalo hunts were over in quantities large enough to last a full year, and so craftily was the task done that neither dog, coyote, or keen-eyed enemy Indian could possibly know where the provisions were stored. A dry spot was selected where the drainage was good. A two-foot circle was marked on the ground and the sod very carefully cut, gently removed and laid aside; then a hole was dug to a depth of two feet at which point it was gradually widened out into a round pit a cross-section of which is shown in Figure 103. The earth was placed on hides and great care taken that none should drop on the grass. When the pit was completed a layer of brush was placed on the bottom and covered with a dry hide, and the sides were also covered with brush and protected with hide. The dried meat and other provisions were placed in the hole and when full a hide was spread over the top together with a quantity of sticks. The hole was then filled with earth tightly packed and the sod very carefully replaced in its original position. The hides containing the earth were then carried down to the river and the dirt thrown in the water, or, if no water was handy, it was hauled some distance away before being scattered on the prairie. If the work were poorly done so that the earth over the cache caved in a little, occasionally the sharp eyes of enemy scouts would spot the pit, but such happenings were rare indeed. Stored in this way, pemmican could be kept safely for at least two years.

COOLERS

Butter, eggs, meat and fresh vegetables must, of course, be kept in a cool place. Two types of coolers are adapted for use in camp—first, those that rely on the coolness of the earth and water, and second, those that rely upon evaporation.

SPRING BOXES

If a lake, stream, or spring is handy the best way to keep food cool is to make a little cellar by sinking a large packing box at a shady place in the bank. In a pit dug to fit at the edge of the water, sink the box to such depth that the water will partially fill it. Shelves should be built around the edge of the box but the center should be left open so that bottles and cans can be submerged in the water. Put a hinged lid on the cooler and

Figure 104. A SPRING BOX

pile rocks on top to prevent animals from intruding. Such a cellar will keep milk, eggs, and meat cool and in good condition much better than one would expect. If no box is handy, the pit may be lined with rock and covered with poles and leafy branches.

In camping where there is no suitable spring or shore, select a shady spot in the heavy woods, dig a square hole in the ground, line it with stone, and place poles and leafy branches over the top, replacing the branches with new ones each day. While such a dry cellar will be many degrees cooler than the surface of the ground, it can be much improved if a packing box is handy by digging the pit a foot larger than the box, and filling in with a six-inch layer of gravel around the sides; when the gravel is moistened with a couple of buckets of water, and a wet burlap thrown over the top protected by green branches, a first-class refrigerator results.

COOLING UNDER WATER

When we are shifting about in the woods and not staying at one place long enough to justify building a refrigerator, the quickest and easiest way to keep food cool is to sink it in the lake or river. Since the butter and lard are usually carried in pails or cans, all that one needs to do is to tie a rope to them and sink them in the water, attaching the other end of the rope to a float to mark the spot. If there are several items, they can be placed in a bag and sunk. If the food does not have sufficient weight to insure it against drifting with the current, a rock may be attached for an anchor, and the food tied to the rope a foot or two above it.

Carefully wrapped in cloth, meat may even be kept for some time by sinking it under water. It is a common practice in the Northwoods to cache fresh meat in winter by sinking it through a hole in the ice, attaching the end of the rope to a stick which will remain exposed and mark the spot after the hole freezes over. This method is used in wolf country where there is fear that the wolves may raid the meat supplies.

COOLING BY EVAPORATION

Here is a principle of refrigeration that every camper should know, and once knowing it, he will certainly employ it often for on the hottest day butter can be kept cool and solid with very little effort. Put the food in a pail, set another pail or a pan filled with water on top of it, and then drape a piece of cheesecloth, burlap, or any other cloth over the top pail so that the center of the cloth may be pushed down into the water, using a rock if necessary to keep it there. The water will soon spread until the cloth is wet and then *the evaporation will keep the food cool and fresh.*

If there is danger of prowling animals getting into the food as it sits on the ground a hole may be dug deep enough so as to accommodate both pails, the cloth draped over them, and the top of the hole then covered with sticks and rocks. Or, with a little ingenuity, the pail of food may be hung from the limb of a tree with a pan of water resting on a board on top of it to keep the cloth wet.

The use of this principle makes it possible to turn the cupboard illustrated in Figure 102 into a refrigerator. Merely put a pan of water on top of it and then drape cheesecloth or burlap over it, with a rock on top to hold it in the water.

Figure 105. A FLOATING COOLER

Another excellent application of this same principle is found in the barrel refrigerator often employed in the lake country of the North, which comes down to us with a long history of use in pioneer times. Attach two boards to the barrel as shown in Figure 105 to keep it from tipping or rolling as it floats in the water, and cut a hole a foot square in the middle of the top side. Anchor the barrel in the lake or river, place the food inside, and lay a piece of burlap or other cloth over the top of the barrel with the ends touching the water. Two factors combine to cool the interior of the barrel, the water below and the evaporation from the cloth above. Frequently such barrel refrigerators are seen attached to the dock by means of a rope, making it possible to pull the barrel in to the dock for securing and replenishing the food supply without the necessity of going out in a boat.

PRESERVING MEAT BY DRYING AND SMOKING

At best refrigeration in the woods is feeble and ineffective, particularly if one is on the go. Of necessity, therefore, the usual method of preserving meat is not by keeping it cool but rather by smoking and drying it. This is true alike of the Indian and white woodsmen. Each has a different method of going about the task and each produces a slightly different product.

The Indian Way—Jerking Meat

The pemmican or jerked meat of the northern Woodland Indians is delicious. I have eaten it many times among the Indians and indeed have made it myself. And wherever one finds it it is not only palatable but refreshing and unusually nourishing. A half a handful is all that one needs for lunch while on the trail and is indeed all that one desires, for a few mouthfuls of this concentrated nutrition seems to satisfy. While the Plains Indians of the old days made the pemmican from buffalo meat, and the Woodland Indians from deer, any kind of meat except pork may be dried in this way, and if well handled the product will keep from three to five years.

First, we need one of the Chippewa kitchens pictured in B and C, Figure 75, in *Camping Crafts*. While this arrangement of poles is used for many purposes around the Chippewa kitchen, its main function is to provide many poles on which to hang the meat while it is drying and smoking. Cut the lean meat up into steaks and strips about a half inch in thickness, crosswise of the grain, and hang them on the framework over the fire. Build a slow, smoldering fire which will throw plenty of smoke and at the same time heat the meat gently. Turn the meat every hour or so and leave it there for three or four days, taking it in at night, the length of time depending somewhat on the weather and the fire. It is a *drying* process rather than a smoking one and if the bright sun hits the rack so much the better. On the prairies the Indians dried the meat without the use of a fire at all. When the meat seems quite thoroughly dried pull it apart with the fingers and pound it with a rock until it is separated into fine bits or shreds.

The jerked meat will now keep indefinitely and can be stored just as it is, but to make real pemmican out of it melted grease must be added. Boil suet, bones, and joints in water as in making soup, let cool and skim off the fat, then heat and pour over the dried meat to the proportion of two parts of meat to one of the fat. The best pemmican is made by boiling out the marrow from a large number of bones rather than using joints with meat attached as in making ordinary soup.

We now have plain pemmican but the Indian would turn it into a more delicious food and a better balanced diet by mixing into it a good quantity of dried chokecherries and even dried blueberries. The Chippewas and their neighbors prized blueberries highly and went great distances to get them, not only because they were considered a delicacy in themselves but were essential for the making of good pemmican.

Fish were dried in this same way, as every fisherman knows who has traveled through the Indian villages of the northern woods in the summer, for there is no more familiar sight than a string of fish hanging over the poles above the campfire in front of the waginogan. If one gives an Indian family a catch of fish that he does not need for his own use, he is pretty sure to find them neatly dressed and hanging over the campfire a half-hour afterwards. But it was among the Indians of the northwest coast that fish were made into pemmican regularly—among the Indians of the northern lake region the more common custom was merely to preserve the fish by drying them, and then to cook them later on when needed.

Explorers going on extended trips into the wilds today frequently prepare a modern pemmican in the city before they start by mixing dried beef, suet and raisins.

A CAMP SMOKEHOUSE

While the Indian's method of jerking meat was more of a drying process, the way of the white pioneer was to smoke it thoroughly. And this calls for a smokehouse of some sort, which takes it somewhat out of the range of a woodcraft or campcraft undertaking, the woodcraft way being more in line with the Indian way. However, a simple smoking arrangement can be quickly rigged up if one has the good fortune to have a barrel and a good-sized packing box at his disposal. In length the packing box should be about twice the diameter of the barrel because the fire must be placed under one end of it so that the heat does not penetrate the barrel and thus reach the meat. Invert the packing box and with an auger bore a number of holes in the bottom of it near one end. The barrel has only one head, and is inverted with the meat suspended from the closed end by strings tied to nails. Invert the barrel over the auger holes in the box, build a little fire in a tin pan or basin, lift up the end of the packing box away from the barrel and slip the pan under it. The smoke will go up through the auger holes into the barrel, and is retained there to smoke the meat. Very little fire is needed and it will not be necessary to replenish it oftener than every hour or two.

Many other smoking arrangements can be rigged up if one uses his ingenuity, but the important thing to remember is that the fire *must be kept away from the meat so that no heat reaches it*, which necessitates building the fire in a separate box of some sort and conducting the smoke into another containing the meat. A stovepipe is frequently used to connect the two.

Not all woods are suitable for smoking meat. Here are three that will not fail—*hickory, hard maple,* and *beech.* In some European countries, red cedar *boughs* are used to give the meat a different flavor than that produced by wood smoke.

BARK-CRAFT

OLD ANIWABI, Medicine Man of the Chippewas, once told me that he hoped that when he reached the Happy Hunting Ground he would find the white birch there. He's there now (may the Great Mystery smile tenderly on his spirit) and let us hope that he is living in a land as richly abounding in glorious birches as were the Northland trails over which he traveled with moccasined feet for close on to a hundred years.

In the culture of the northern Woodland Indians, the white birch was well nigh an indispensable factor. It not only added a lovely lace-like touch of beauty amid the evergreens along the banks of lakes and rivers, but its sap supplied the foundation for a delicious syrup, its inner bark an edible flour for emergency use—and so, in the eternal struggle with the Hunger Demon the danger of complete defeat was small for those who dwelt in White Birch Land; nor was there great danger from the Frost Fiend, for the wood of the birch offered long-lived and coal-producing fuel for campfires, and sturdy staves of it made the finest frames for snowshoes.

But the crowning gift of this precious tree, surpassing all others and reducing them to insignificance, is its outer bark. *Birch-bark*—the Woods Indian's parfleche, his leather, his parchment, his wrapping paper, his canvas, his tin—thick, pliable, leather-like, waterproof, decay-proof, insect-proof, destructible only by fire! From it the Indian obtained tinder for campfires more inflammable than paper and long burning from the generous oil within, roofs for wigwams that withstood the storms for years upon years, feather-weight baskets for his food and berries, waterproof pots and kettles for his cooking, and

21

as the pinnacle of queenly gifts, *covering for the lightest and most buoyant of canoes*. Were it not for birch-bark the chances are that the Redman would not have given to the civilized world his greatest contribution, the canoe—and that indeed would have been a loss beyond the power of words to portray.

There were other barks invaluable to the Indian in the work-a-day life of fashioning an existence out of the materials the woods produced, such as white cedar, spruce, basswood, elm, and hemlock, but none was comparable to birch-bark in the variety of needs to which it administered.

A knowledge of the uses of birch and other barks is an important asset in the life of the wilds; the skills of bark-craft will not only be interesting to all who seek to know woodland ways, but will be valuable on countless occasions in the course of extended camping trips in the bush. Moreover, of all the types of crafts growing out of materials found in the woods, bark-craft has proven to be one of the most fascinating to boys and girls, and this being the case, it is an excellent activity for the woodcraft department of an organized camp—it is completely and inseparably related to the woods and utilizes none but materials the bush provides.

But like so many good things, there may be unhappy consequences in the extensive use of bark-craft, particularly if good judgment is not at the paddle. Wherever one goes in the resort woodlands of the North, ugly, black scars stare him in the face from the once beautiful trunks of lovely birches, scars that will remain as eyesores as long as stand the trees, perpetually publishing the selfishness of unscrupulous campers or the ignorance of tenderfeet. No craft is worth such destruction of the beauty and usefulness of the woods. But fortunately bark in sufficient quantities can usually be obtained without marring the scenery in the slightest and without injuring the stand of birches.

If only a small amount of bark is needed for two or three baskets, it may frequently be obtained from a fallen tree or a dead standing tree; almost decay-proof as it is, it is no unusual thing to find the bark sound and entirely acceptable on an old log the wood of which has almost completely rotted away. (In fact, so completely does the sound bark on a fallen tree camouflage the condition of the log within that *it would be folly indeed ever to cross a stream on a fallen birch log*, especially with a pack on your back, for you might be treacherously dumped into the water as the rotted log gives way—to the seasoned woodsman the sight of birch-bark on a log across a stream spells *danger!*) Failing to find a fallen log, a little scouting around may discover birches growing in a clump, several arising from the same roots in the way that these trees are wont to do in cut-over regions, one or two of which can be dropped to the benefit of the remainder.

The problem becomes one of concern only when large quantities of bark are needed, as would be the case for the instructional program in woodcraft or campcraft in an organized camp featuring bark-craft. Is it ever permissible for the campers in such camps to gather their own bark in the large volumes required? If the camp is situated in the far and remote wilds with lumbering areas near enough at hand to be accessible, then there is no reason why the campers should not be transported to the suitable regions and, under the supervision of woodsmen, enjoy the valuable experience of barking, following the instructions given in the section which follows in this chapter. But this should not be permitted except under informed adult guidance, and under no circumstances should it be considered in other areas than those suitable for lumbering.

Camps not fortunate enough to have access to uninhabited wilderness should purchase the bark. Wholesale florist-supply companies usually sell birch-bark suitable for small projects, but the sheets often run a little small for the various uses the craft demands. The best plan is to order it from a guide, Indian, or lumberjack in the northern woods—he will select it intelligently, sending heavy bark in large sheets and doing no damage to the woods in securing it. In this connection, it should be said that the average Woodland Indian knows the barking game better than all others, since bark-craft is a time-honored skill of his people.

The stripping of bark all the way around a young birch tree will usually kill the tree, but not so with large and old trees; new bark will soon form, even though it be black and rough, and the tree will continue to prosper. One frequently sees huge birches in the Northwoods with dark areas which indicate unmistakably where the expert hands of Indians removed large sheets of bark in long years past. Even if the removing of bark from young trees did no damage whatever, not even to the appearance of the tree, there would be no point in taking it since it would be too thin to be put to any constructive use—that needed is the thick, heavy bark of old trees. The only permanent damage done to the large birch trees by stripping the bark is that the dark, rough bark that replaces the original is not so pleasing to the eye; but if the stripping is done in a lumbering area, these large trees will soon be dropped anyway, or if taken in the remote woods, the old trees will probably fall of their own accord long before a resort development takes place if indeed it ever does.

The thought of stripping birch trees is repellent to many, owing to the unrestrained proclivity of tourists in this direction in the camping and park areas, but to object to it under the circumstances recommended herewith, is to indicate a lack of familiarity with the overabundance of the untracked wilderness and the methods of the lumbering country. *True conservation means intelligent use.*

Experience has indicated that campers who have become acquainted with bark-craft under proper guidance are much less inclined to strip bark from birch trees promiscuously, than are the uninitiated, owing to the fact that they are fully familiar with all the hazards from every angle.

So write to some one in the remote bush and have him secure a goodly supply of bark and ship it—the only expense will be the cost of the labor and the shipping, in all probability, because the bark itself usually costs nothing.

GETTING THE BIRCH-BARK

Granted that the conditions under which it is permissible to remove bark, as set forth in the preceding pages, are fully met, then we are ready for the interesting woodcraft experience of barking, which, by the way, involves somewhat of an art.

Bark can be successfully stripped only in the spring and early summer. At these times of the year it is frequently so loose that it springs from the tree of its own accord with a sudden ripping sound once it has been slit down one side of the trunk. With the coming of hot summer weather (the time varying with the locality and the nature of the season), it clings to the tree with such tenacity that it can be removed only with great difficulty and often cannot be successfully removed at all. Needs should be anticipated and a sufficient supply secured in the spring or early summer.

Large trees do not necessarily have thick, heavy bark. One is frequently disappointed to find that the bark from a big tree, although clean and beautiful in appearance, is so thin as to be worthless. Before attempting to remove the bark, chip into it with the point of a camp-ax, thus prying loose a little corner, and feel of it—if it is not of sufficient thickness, move along to another tree.

A camp-ax is the only really essential tool needed to strip the bark. Having selected a tree at least eight inches in diameter and preferably larger, cut the bark in a straight, vertical line from as high up as you

Figure 106. STRIPPING BIRCH-BARK

can reach down to a point near the ground, as indicated in A, Figure 106. Strike firmly straight into the tree with the full blade of the ax—there is little danger of cutting through into the wood. Then insert the fingers into the slit made by the ax, and work the sheet loose around the tree. It should peel very easily and readily, but if it tends to stick, work gently with the fingers so as not to split or crack the sheet.

The removing of bark in this way frequently makes the fingers sore and bruised. If much bark is to be taken, a wooden spud of hard wood, similar to that shown in C, Figure 106, will be a great convenience, the spud serving to pry the bark loose and thus protecting the fingers. After the bark has been slit with the ax, slip the broad edge of the spud under it and work it loose. The spud is made from a stick two feet long and three inches thick.

Bark will usually stick to the tree trunk at those points where large black spots or old knots appear on the white surface. To attempt to force it loose from these spots will result in splitting the bark or leaving a hole, thus rendering the sheet useless. To prevent this, the black spot should be well but gently pounded with the handle of the spud or with the ax, as indicated in B, Figure 106, the pounding tending to loosen the bark so that it can be pried free without splitting.

The foregoing instructions are given on the assumption that it is not wise to fell the tree. Of course, if the tree can be dropped, several good sheets can be secured from it rather than just one, and this is often better than to meddle with several trees. That is the way the Chippewa Indian would work—he would fell the tree and strip the bark in large sheets from the entire length of its trunk. Do not chop the tree without the consent of the owner and the advice of those who know, but if it seems wise, take all the bark that is thick enough, and then return later and split up the trunk into firewood.

Carrying the Storing Bark

When a supply of birch-bark has been cut it should be rolled into bundles and tied. Roll one sheet, then roll another around it, and so on until a bundle of convenient size for carrying has been made, as illustrated in D, Figure 106. When a sheet of newly cut bark is laid on the ground, it will retain the curve it had on the tree and thus curl up. In rolling the bark, *never roll it with this natural curve*, that is, *do not roll it with the white side out*. If this is done it will be found, on unrolling the bundle, that the natural curve will be so set and the edges so curled as to render the sheets useless. Rather, roll it against the natural curve, with the brown side out, or roll it sideways to the natural curve.

With the bark on location, it should be unrolled immediately and the sheets piled flat on the ground in a shady place, with the brown side down. Place some logs or rocks on top of the pile to keep the sheets flat, taking care to place weights along the edges to prevent them from curling. The bark will absorb moisture from the ground and thus keep its natural pliable quality much longer than if stored in a building.

Birch-bark will resist decay for an unbelievably long period. I once saw a pile of birch-bark shingles in Canada which were removed from a barn that had been built seventy years before and was so dilapidated that it had to be wrecked. The shingles were in as good shape as the day they were put on the building, and were stored away to be used on the new building when it was erected.

So we need have no fear of decay in leaving the bark on the ground, but if it is to be kept for a long period, say for the next season, as is often the case when a supply is left over at the end of the summer, it would be better to store it in a building. Lay it flat on the floor with weights on it. When it is taken out for use, it should again be placed on the ground in a damp, shady place.

If a piece of bark proves to be too stiff and brittle when needed, it is because it has dried out too much. All that is required to put it in shape is to soak it for a little while in water.

OTHER KINDS OF BARK

If birch-bark is not available, one of the following barks may be substituted: *elm, basswood, poplar, cottonwood,* or *wild cherry root.* Many of the projects described in this chapter may be made from any of these. Each of them has characteristics of its own, reacting in different ways to handling, and making differently appearing products, but each will be found to be reasonably successful for most types of bark-craft. For small articles, bark from the large roots of wild cherry has a most satisfying appearance, resembling birch-bark in tone and vying with it in beauty. It goes without saying, however, that no material in the woods is quite comparable to birch-bark either in the ease with which it can be worked or in the lightness, strength, and durability of the finished product. It is in a class all its own, but when it cannot be obtained there is no need of abandoning bark-craft—use one of the other barks.

LACINGS FOR BARK-CRAFT

Lacings of some sort are needed with which to fasten the sheets of bark together and to tie them to the framework of the article under construction. Two styles of materials may be used here—"civilized" materials such as cord, yarn, and thread, or natural lacings, found in the woods.

Although a modern product of the white man, colored yarn is a very effective lacing for small birch-bark projects and gives a delightful Indian touch. In recent years the Indians have developed a fondness for colored yarn and use it extensively for many types of crafts. Little baskets, napkin-rings, fans, and similar small bark articles are particularly attractive when laced with blue and red yarn. The yarn seems to give a primitive touch and fits the picture better than one would imagine. The woods-dwelling Indians sometimes lace their small bark articles with natural lacings and then decorate them with simple designs put on with yarn.

Those possessed of the true woodcraft spirit, however, will prefer lacings made of woods materials. These are obtained from basswood and other barks, and from certain roots:

Basswood-Bark Lacings.—The *wigub* or bark lacings of the Chippewas, pliable, tough, and exceedingly strong, are made from the inner bark of basswood in the great majority of cases. In fact the word *wigub* while referring in exact meaning to all kinds of bark lacings, means basswood thongs to the average Chippewa, so universally are they used and so superior are they considered to those of other possible materials. For use in bark-craft, basswood lacings are to be preferred to all others.

Basswood bark should be taken in narrow strips from up the side of the tree rather than by removing it all the way around the trunk. The taking of these narrow vertical strips does not affect the life of the tree. With a hand-ax, loosen a piece of bark about four inches wide near the bottom of the tree as indicated in A, Figure 107, take this end in the hands, and tear the strip loose as far up the tree trunk as possible by pulling outward and away from the tree. Often a strip fifteen or twenty feet long may be obtained in this way. As the strip is pulled loose it usually becomes narrower and narrower in width, and thus frees itself from the tree far above one's head. Do not take more than two such strips from one tree. Roll up each strip as it is removed into a convenient bundle to carry back to camp, as shown in C, Figure 107.

The lacings are made from the inner layer of the bark and consequently the woody outer surface must now be removed. If we would accomplish this with the greatest ease, we will take our lesson from the woodsy-wise Chippewa and cut the strips in lengths of about five feet, place them under water at the edge of the lake properly weighted with stones, there to leave them for about ten days. Soft and slippery when taken out, the yellow inner bark can be peeled from the rough outer layer with no effort at all. Should the lacings be needed at once, the ten-day soaking period may be dispensed with and the two layers separated on the day the bark is stripped from the tree: grasp the strip in the hands at its middle with the outer side up and bend sharply downward, as illustrated in B, Figure 107, thus breaking the woody outer layer which is then pulled loose and discarded. However, the greater ease with which the well-soaked bark is

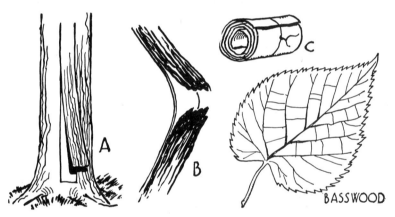

Figure 107. STRIPPING BASSWOOD BARK FOR LACINGS

separated, and the superior smoothness of the strands resulting, admonish us to separate only that which is needed on the day the bark is removed and soak the remainder a full ten days.

The wigub we shall need are thin flat strands one-eighth to three-sixteenths of an inch in width, and four to five feet long. The soft, slippery inner fiber as it is removed after the ten-day soaking is in ideal condition to be stripped into these slender strands. Merely run the finger nail down it, taking off strands of the desired width. A little difficulty may be encountered in securing lacings of uniform width and thickness, but in common with all woodcraft projects, a woodsy, irregular and handmade appearance is expected and desired in bark articles and therefore absolutely accurate lacings are not necessary nor are they possible. When enough lacings have been stripped for our immediate needs, the remainder of the pieces of inner fiber may be rolled into bundles and saved, to be well soaked again when it is desired to strip them into strands.

Now the inner layer of bark of basswood consists of many layers of fiber and it can be separated into sheets as thin as paper or left at its full thickness, depending on the strength of cord desired. It is better to leave it at its full thickness, merely stripping it into strands of the desired width, and to make it thinner if need be at the time it is actually applied to the article under construction. To make the wigub thinner, take the soaked strand in the hands at its middle and bend it sharply downward, thus loosening the layers so that they can be stripped loose with the finger nail.

These bark lacings should be hung up until needed, and before being used should be soaked for a few hours in water. Unless soaked, they will be stiff and will break easily.

Other Bark Lacings.—Slippery-elm bark is the nearest approach to basswood bark and is the choice of the Chippewas when basswood is not at hand. Its inner bark can be separated from the outer very easily without the necessity of soaking as in the case of basswood.

Other barks usable for lacings are: *hickory, white oak, red cedar, osage-orange,* and *buckeye.* The inner bark is used in each case and the lacings are prepared in essentially the same way as described for basswood bark.

*Root Lacings.—*Another source of lacings is found in the trailing roots of *spruce, tamarack, hemlock, red cedar* and *cottonwood.* Of these, spruce and hemlock were most commonly used by the Woodland Indians, these being unusually strong and pliable. Such root cordage is called *wadub* by the Chippewas but is sometimes referred to as *watab* by the white folks of the woods. Although these root lacings were sometimes used in making canoes and baskets, they were usually a second choice to basswood bark both from the standpoint of convenience and neatness of appearance.

Secure the trailing rootlets near the surface of the ground under spruce or other trees mentioned. Remove the bark and soak the roots in water. Very slender rootlets may be used just as they are, but the usual procedure is to select roots about the size of a pencil and quarter them.

Coloring the Lacings.—The basswood-bark lacings may be applied to baskets in their natural color or they may be dyed in any shade desired. Uncolored, the lacings give the article a natural, woodsy appearance, but most people prefer the contrast of another color against the brown and white of the birch-bark.

Color the lacings in ordinary dye in the same way that cloth would be dyed. Blue, red, and green are the best colors to use on birch-bark.

FUNDAMENTALS OF WORKING WITH BIRCH-BARK

The following tools are all that are needed in working with birch-bark: *tin-shears, jackknife, ice-pick,* and *darning needles.*

A pair of tin-shears is the ideal tool for cutting the bark. Thick birch-bark is very tough and difficult to cut with any other tool. Straight cuts and curves can be executed quickly and easily with the tin-snips.

If a jackknife must be used, the sheet of bark should not be laid down and the knife drawn across it as in cutting cardboard, but rather, a line should be drawn on the bark with a pencil and then the bark should be picked up and cut. The blade cannot be placed at right angles to the edge of the bark, however, but should be held at an angle of about forty-five degrees, as illustrated in E, Figure 112. At this angle a sharp knife will cut the bark, but regardless of how efficient one may be with a knife, he will welcome the tin-shears if he has much cutting to do.

Holes for the lacings may be punched in the bark with an ice-pick, awl, or similar sharp-pointed instrument. A good punching tool for this purpose can be easily made from materials found at hand—from a branch of white cedar about an inch and a half in thickness, cut a section four inches long; into the end of it drive a nail, cut off the head, and sharpen the end with a file. G in Figure 111 shows the finished tool. The Woodland Indians employed for this purpose a sharply pointed bone, often a deer splint, with the handle made by wrapping the bone with buckskin—this was called a *canoe awl* because of its use in making birch-bark canoes.

To punch the bark, force the tool through with a gentle, twisting motion; if the bark is in good condition, it will take a clean, round hole without splitting. Should it tend to split regularly when punched, obviously the bark is too dry and should be soaked.

Yarn is applied to birch-bark with a darning needle.

If two sheets of bark are to be laced together, small wooden pegs are needed to hold them in place while the lacings are applied. F in Figure 111 illustrates these pegs—they are about two inches long. As each hole is punched through the two sheets with the ice-pick, a peg is inserted to hold the sheets together temporarily. The pegs are removed as the lacing progresses.

In practically all kinds of birch-bark work, the inner or brown side of the bark should be placed out. White men are usually inclined to want to put the white side of the bark out, but not so with the Indians! The inner or brown side is firmer and more durable, withstanding the wear and tear much better, and will not peel. In the long run it will be found more attractive—one does not tire of it so quickly. This is not a hard and fast rule, for occasional objects are made with the white side out, but it is nevertheless the safe course to follow always. Certain it is that for all uses where the bark is to come in contact with the elements, the brown side should be on the exposed surface. The only Chippewa makuks (baskets) with the brown surface inside were the pitch baskets for pine pitch, the grease buckets, and some syrup containers, the reason for putting the firmer surface inside in these cases being obvious.

SIMPLE BIRCH-BARK PROJECTS

As our introduction to bark-craft, let us fashion a few simple articles such as napkin-rings, place-cards, hot plates, and fans, which will serve to familiarize us with the techniques of working with bark and prepare us for the larger and more characteristic bark projects.

Bark Napkin-Rings

Although in no respect related to the type of life lived in the woods or to the culture of primitives, napkin-rings serve as an excellent introduction to birch-bark craft. They are simple and delightful projects for young campers.

From a comparatively thin piece of bark, cut a strip one-and-three-fourths inches wide and seven inches long. Curl it into the shape of a napkin-ring with the brown side out, overlapping the ends about a half inch; then punch a hole through the two layers of bark with the ice-pick and insert a wooden peg into the hole to hold the ring together temporarily. Now punch a row of holes a half inch apart through the two layers across the width of the napkin-ring, and lace the two layers together with a narrow thong of well-soaked basswood bark or with yarn, as shown in A, Figure 108. In this simplest type of ring, the edges of the bark are left uncovered and unprotected, but a decorative zigzag of red or blue yarn may well be sewed near such edge, as indicated in A.

Grass-edged Napkin-Ring.—A more finished and attractive napkin-ring is illustrated in B, Figure 108. Over the edges of the strip of bark place a few strands of grass, preferably sweet grass, and sew in

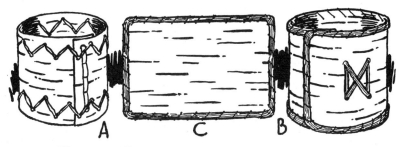

Figure 108. BIRCH-BARK NAPKIN-RINGS AND PLACE-CARD

place with black thread as illustrated. The sweet grass is desirable because of the delightful perfume which it retains permanently. When the edging is completed, curl the strip of bark into the ring and sew the overlapping ends together with thread. Complete the ring by sewing one or two simple designs on the sides with red or blue yarn or with porcupine quills. The designs should be small, not over a half inch across, and should be very simple—a cross, an X, or a Z. Always avoid initials and white-man symbols.

Another excellent edging is found in a thin strip cut from a cat-tail leaf. It is easier than grass to handle and apply, and turns dark with time, giving a nice contrast against the light brown of the bark.

Spiral Napkin-Rings.—Spiral napkin-rings are always popular since they are not only decorative in appearance but are easy to make, requiring no sewing or lacing. To make the ring illustrated in B, Figure 109, cut a piece of thin bark in the shape shown in A, two-and-a-half inches wide and twenty-three inches long. For six inches it remains at full width, and then tapers gradually to the end. Coil the wide end into a ring two inches in diameter and then roll the remainder of the strip around it, and make secure by inserting the narrow tip into a little slit cut in the layer beneath, as illustrated in B.

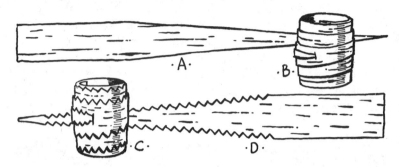

Figure 109. SPIRAL NAPKIN-RINGS

The ring shown in C, Figure 109, is made in much the same way. The layout of the bark strip is shown in D.

BIRCH-BARK PLACE-CARDS

Place-cards of birch-bark are particularly appropriate for camp reunions and banquets of outdoor organizations. From a thin piece of bark, cut two cards two by three-and-one-half inches in size. One of these cards should be cut so that the grain of the bark goes lengthwise and the other so that it goes crosswise. Place the two cards together with the brown side out in each case, cover the edges with a few strands of sweet grass or a strip of cattail leaf (as described for napkin-rings above), and sew together with black thread. The completed card is shown in C, Figure 108.

One can write with pen and ink on birch-bark as easily as on paper. The bark also takes water colors nicely—so painted symbols or decorations may be added if desired.

BIRCH-BARK HOT-PLATES

Hot-plates for use on the table under hot dishes are illustrated in Figure 110. Each is made of two layers of bark, so placed that the grain of one goes at right angles to the grain of the other, each with the brown side out. A single layer of bark will warp if used for this purpose. The edges may be laced together with colored yarn or basswood bark as shown in A and B, or they may be covered with sweet grass or strips of cattail leaf and sewed with black thread as in C.

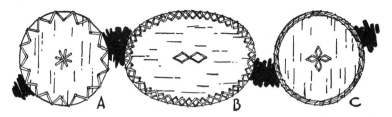

Figure 110. BIRCH-BARK HOT-PLATES

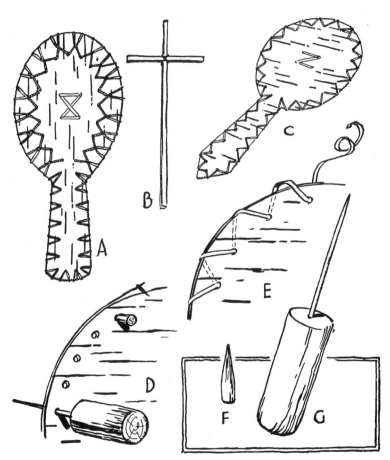

Figure 111. INDIAN BIRCH-BARK FANS

Birch-Bark Fans

The birch-bark fans of the Woods-dwelling Indians were used for the same purpose for which fans are used today, and were also carried while dancing. In these dances the Redmen would step forth strenuously for a few minutes and then rest for a while by dancing quietly and leisurely, fanning themselves the while both for the purpose of cooling themselves and of adding to the colorful spectacle of the dance, the fan being moved to the rhythm of the drumming. In story dances, the fan would often be used for an eye-shade in the dramatic method of looking at a supposedly distant object. Fans made from eagle wings were used in the same way.

First make the cross shown in B, Figure 111, by whittling two slender sticks from a splinter of cedar or other soft wood and tying together—this is for the purpose of giving rigidity to the fan. The cross should be fourteen inches long and six inches wide. Then cut out two pieces of thick bark in the shape of the fan, fourteen-and-one-half inches long and seven inches wide for the fan shown in A, or eight-and-one-fourth inches wide for C.

Place the cross between the two layers of bark, the brown side of the bark being out. With an ice-pick, punch a hole through the two layers at the top, bottom, and each side of the fan, and through each hole insert a wooden peg similar to that shown in F—these pegs hold the bark in place while it is being laced. Now punch holes all the way around the fan, three-fourths of an inch apart and a half inch in from the edge, and through these holes run red and blue yarn by means of a darning-needle, sewing the two layers of bark together with a decorative edge as in A and C. A simple design should also be placed in the center with yarn. Basswood lacings may be used instead of yarn, but the yarn is quite effective on fans. Other styles of fans may be easily worked out.

BIRCH-BARK BASKETS

Now we come to the making of the beautiful birch-bark makuks of the Indians of the northern woodlands, so interesting as wood-craft projects, so useful in the life of the woods, and so appropriate in camps, cabins and dens. In endless variety these baskets appear among the Indians, particularly the Chippewas who are the masters of bark-craft, but an analysis of them indicates that they are all of a few general types. These we shall consider in the pages that follow, adhering strictly to the Indian patterns and methods of construction. It should be remembered that in recent years the Indians have supplemented their traditional styles of baskets with other shapes designed to satisfy the white man's needs, as for example, the waste-basket, but in making even these modern shapes, they have adhered to the time-honored methods of their fathers. Both the traditional and the modern shapes we shall describe.

We shall discuss the making of the first basket in complete detail and thereafter go into detail only when the baskets differ from the methods used in the first.

Some baskets are made from a single sheet of bark, others from two or more pieces:

Baskets Made from a Single Sheet of Bark

The old baskets of the Chippewas were nearly always made from a single sheet of bark folded up and bound into form. In the pages that follow are described these sturdy work baskets of the Red woodsmen of long years past—plain, substantial makuks that will stand up under the rigors of the day's work, and delicate, fancy ones that combine ornamentation with usefulness.

Square and Rectangular Baskets.—A standard basket of the ancient pattern is shown in A, Figure 112. This is a square basket—rectangular baskets of similar construction are shown in F, Figure 112, and in A, Figure 114, each accompanied by its pattern. Let us consider the making of the square basket (A, Figure 112) in full detail, and from these instructions the methods of fashioning the others can be easily worked out.

The pattern for the basket is shown in B, Figure 112. Cut this pattern from cardboard in the dimensions shown, place it on the birch-bark, and mark the outline on the bark with a pencil. Cut out the bark along the lines with a pair of tin-shears or a sharp jackknife. Remember that in order to cut the bark with a knife the blade must be held at an angle of at least 45 degrees to the edge of the bark, as shown in E, Figure 112.

The dotted lines on the pattern indicate the lines where the bark is to be bent. Place a straight-edge on these lines and run a sharp instrument such as the ice-pick over them, thus making a slight crease so that the bark will bend readily and evenly.

It will be noted in the pattern shown in B that there is a V-shaped section at each end of the basket. Bend up these V's first, then bend up the sides and fold the square end-pieces around outside the V-shaped sections. Punch two holes through the layers of bark at each end with an ice-pick or awl and insert wooden pegs to hold all in place temporarily, as shown in D, Figure 112.

Now a "hoop" must be whittled for the top of the basket, similar to that shown in C, Figure 112. This is made from a stick cut from a white-cedar strip, or from a small branch of green maple or ash. The stick should be about a quarter of an inch in diameter, and uniform throughout. If the stick is from a cedar board it may be a thin, rectangular strip, but if from a maple branch it may either be left round, whittled to about the thickness of a lead pencil throughout, or the round stick may be split in half. Soak the stick in water and then bend it into the square or rectangular shape to fit the top of the basket. Of course the corners will be rounded and at best it will be a very irregular square or rectangle, and sometimes the result may be more of an oval, but with care reasonably straight sides can be produced as shown in C. Thin down the ends where they overlap and lash together by wrapping them for a distance of at least two inches with a well-soaked thong of basswood bark, as shown in C, Figure 112. If the hoop is a little too large or too small when placed on the basket, its size can easily be changed by shoving the ends together or pulling them apart. The making of the hoop is by far the most difficult part of constructing a basket, and special pains should be taken with it, whittling it here and there and experimenting until it takes on the shape of the basket top.

Place the hoop around the top of the basket *outside* the bark, punch holes through the bark just below it in three or four places, and tie it in place temporarily, as shown in D. Be sure that the hoop is parallel to the table as the basket sits in its natural position, then trim off the bark evenly along the top edge of the hoop. Then punch holes with an ice-pick every three-fourths inch all the way around the top of the basket, and lace the hoop firmly in place as shown in A, Figure 112, using yarn if necessary but preferably thongs of basswood bark well soaked to make them pliable (see page 28, for instructions for making basswood thongs). While plain basswood strands may be used, better effects are produced if they are dyed green, red, or blue. When the end of the thong is reached, wrap it around three times

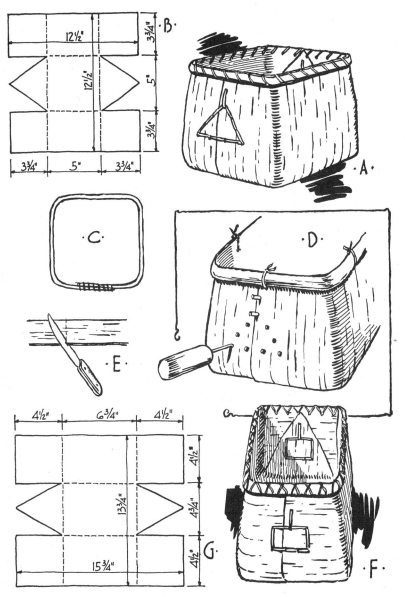

Figure 112. SQUARE AND RECTANGULAR BASKETS OF BIRCH-BARK

through the same hole and tuck the end under the loops thus formed.

With the hoop lashed in place, complete the basket by fastening together the layers of bark at the ends, using either the triangular arrangement of holes shown in A, Figure 112, or the rectangular one shown in F.

In making baskets it is particularly important that the brown side of the bark be placed on the outside.

The rectangular basket shown in F is made in exactly the same way as the square one just described. In A, Figure 114, however, we have a basket made with rectangular end pieces rather than triangular ones. Its pattern is shown in B.

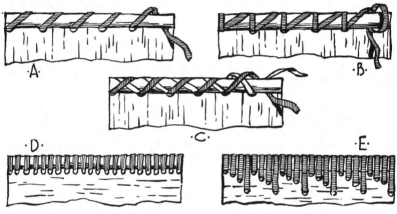

Figure 113. BORDERS FOR BIRCH-BARK MAKUKS

These are all sturdy, strong makuks of the type that did heavy service in the Indian wigwams of long years past. What they may lack in ornamentation and decorative quality is made up by their serviceability. They may easily be turned into fancy baskets, however, by using one of the ornamental borders in colored lacings described in the sections following.

Methods of Lacing the Hoop Border.—Figure 113 shows five lacings used by the Chippewa Indians in binding the hoop to the top of the basket.

That shown in A is the simplest of the lacings—it appears on the basket pictured in A, Figure 112. It is commonly used on all small baskets where ornamentation is not the goal.

In large baskets where strength is demanded the lacing shown in B is frequently employed by the Indians. The drawing clearly illustrates the method of applying it and its appearance on the basket is seen in A, Figure 114 and in Figure 121.

The double lacing in C makes a strong and more durable basket and at the same time a more attractive one. It appears on the baskets in D, Figure 119 and in C, Figure 114.

In the lacing shown in D the basswood thongs are placed so close together that they touch each other. This makes a solid, smooth border for the basket, and a very ornamental one if colored lacings that contrast with the birch-bark are used. We see this on the basket in Figure 118.

On fancy baskets the lacing shown in E is a Chippewa favorite. It gives the basket a delightful and truly Indian atmosphere, particularly if colored lacings are used. This method is not recommended for baskets that are to be subjected to rough usage but is unexcelled when ornamentation is desired. It appears on the baskets in Figures 116 and 117.

Flat Trays.—The low, flat basket illustrated in E, Figure 114 is an appropriate paper tray in which to keep correspondence on the desk in rustic camp offices and dens, and is often pressed into service as a bread basket in camps and resorts. The tray measures nine-and-one-half by twelve inches and is made in precisely the same way as the square and rectangular baskets described above. The pattern is indicated in F.

Huge baskets of this pattern measuring twenty-four to thirty inches in length and five inches in depth are used by the Chippewa Indians during the wild-rice harvest and are called *nosa'tcina'gûn* or *winnowing trays;* after the rice has been parched in huge kettles and trodden in a barrel sunk in the ground, it is placed in these winnowing trays and tossed in the air to free it from the chaff.

Baskets with Oval Tops.—C in Figure 114 illustrates a rectangular basket with an oval top. These baskets are usually a little wider at the bottom than at the top. They are made just as described for the square and rectangular baskets above except that the hoop for the top is made oblong in shape, and the bark is forced in at the top so as to take the shape of the hoop, the bark at the ends being trimmed accordingly. Of course the so-called rectangular baskets may be more oval than rectangular at the top, owing to the difficulty in

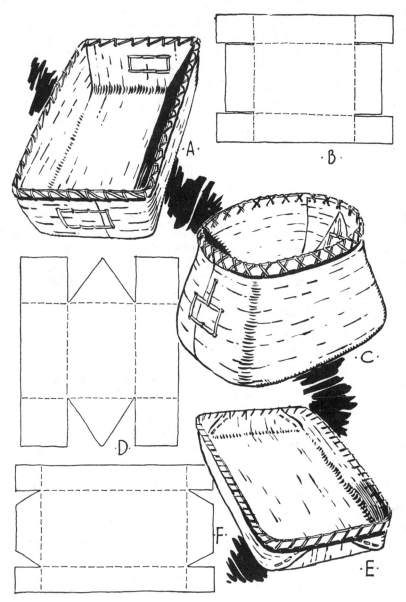

Figure 114.

bending the hoop, but in this basket the aim is to make the top a perfect oval.

Baskets with Shoulder Straps.—A basket to hang on one's shoulder for gathering berries and the like is shown in A, Figure 115. The method of construction is the same as in the case of the square and rectangular baskets described above, except that the top is drawn in and made two or three inches smaller than the base, and the ends are laced in a more substantial way. The bark should be cut according

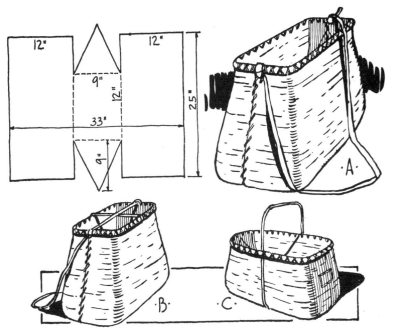

Figure 115. CARRYING BASKETS AND FISH CREELS

to the pattern, and when the sides are bent up into the shape of the basket the end pieces should be trimmed roughly to fit together as in A. In all baskets of these types the ends should be pegged temporarily at the start but the final lacing should be reserved for the last process in completing the basket. When the hoop has been firmly laced in place, then the trimming of the end pieces can be carefully completed so that they fit snugly together and can be laced as shown in the drawing.

The shoulder strap consists of the two-inch strip of basswood bark or heavy buckskin, tied to the hoop at each end of the basket.

A Trout Creel.—Light in weight, strong and serviceable, a creel of birch-bark would satisfy the most discriminating of trout fishermen. It is made exactly like the basket with shoulder straps just described, except smaller in size—ten inches long, five inches wide, and six or seven inches high. A cover or lid is unnecessary—all that is needed is two strips of basswood-bark an inch or two in width, tied across the top as shown in B, Figure 115.

A Hand Basket.—Although no Indian model, a handle added to one of the rectangular baskets described above creates the hand basket

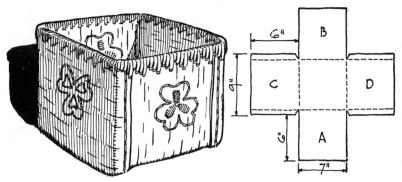

Figure 116. FANCY SQUARE BASKET

illustrated in C, Figure 115. The handle may be made from a thin strip of white cedar or black ash, or from a heavy strip of basswood-bark. The making of the ash strips used by the Indians in constructing ash baskets is rather difficult to the uninitiated, and the novice will find it more convenient to whittle a thin strip of white cedar, soak it well, and bend it into the shape of the handle. The handle is inserted between the hoop and the bark, and extends all the way around the basket, the ends being overlapped and tied at the bottom.

Fancy Square Baskets.—No better container for mother's thread, thimbles, scissors, and darning needles could be desired than the fancy square basket set forth in Figure 116. Designed as it is to hold small objects, it is not constructed so substantially as those previously described, but it is lighter in weight and more attractive.

Note in the pattern that the side sections C and D are wider than

A and B—this is to provide an overlapping edge of one inch 'for the lacing when the sides are folded up. First run a pointed instrument along the dotted lines to crease the bark so that it will bend evenly. Double up the sides A and B, then bend up the sides C and D, and fold the one-inch extensions around the corners. Punch a hole through the two layers of bark at the top and bottom of each of these corners and insert small pegs to hold the basket in shape temporarily while the "hoop" is being laced in place.

A very slender and pliable stick not over one-eighth to three-sixteenths inch in diameter is used for the top of this type of basket—a willow branch or a thin strip of cedar; or if you have no objection to "civilized" materials a piece of wire is excellent—the wire facilitates the making of the square corners shown in the basket in the illustration. Place the stick or wire around the top edge of the bark on the outside of the basket, punch an occasional hole and tie it temporarily. The ends of the "hoop" should not overlap but should be trimmed just to meet each other. Now proceed to lace the "hoop" permanently, using the fancy stitch shown in Figure 116, and set forth in detail in E, Figure 113, punching the holes through the bark as needed with an ice-pick. In the interest of an attractive job the basswood-bark thongs used should be of uniform width and should be dyed dark green.

With the top border completed, all that remains is to lace up the four corners permanently by punching holes every half inch through the overlapped corners and lacing securely as shown. The designs on the sides of the basket are applied with slender thongs of basswood-bark dyed green and red.

Figure 117 shows another very beautiful basket with a square bottom and a circular top. Its pattern is shown in A and the method of construction is similar to that of the basket just described. The narrow sides are bent up first and then the wide sides are folded up and the extensions at the edges lapped over the corners and pegged temporarily. These extensions should extend over the underlying bark one-half inch. The result of this procedure should be a basket that has a circular top. A slender green stick is next bent around the top and laced to it in the usual fashion, using the fancy lacing illustrated in E, Figure 113. The basswood-bark thongs should be dyed dark green or red.

The decorations on the sides of this basket are made by scraping the bark following the instructions on page 55, "Decorating Birch-bark Baskets."

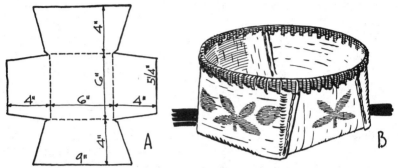

Figure 117. A Fancy Basket with Square Bottom and Circular Top

Fancy Basket with Cover.—The delightful little makuk with the cover shown in Figure 118 is very similar in construction to the one

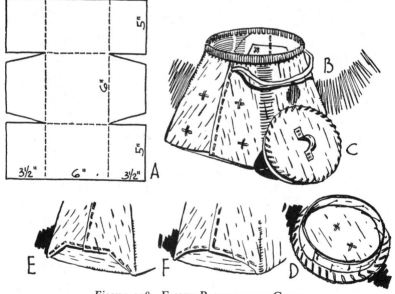

Figure 118. Fancy Basket with Cover

last described. It makes a most acceptable little sewing basket or gadget container. The pattern is shown in A—a piece of medium heavy, clean bark is needed, measuring 13 by 16 inches. When cut as indicated in A and folded up as in B, a basket will result measuring six inches in height with a square, six-inch bottom, and a circular top five inches in diameter. The stitch shown in D, Figure 113 is used around the top. The lacing holding the layers of bark at the sides should run perpendicular to the bottom edge of the basket, going up the middle of the side, and the excess bark on the outside layer should be trimmed off close to it. The handle is of buckskin, attached by running the ends through holes a half inch from the top, a knot being tied at each end to prevent its pulling out.

The cover is shown in C and D. It is made of two pieces sewed together with thread, and a handle of bark attached with basswood lacings as shown. The colored bark lacings around the edge of the cover are for decoration only.

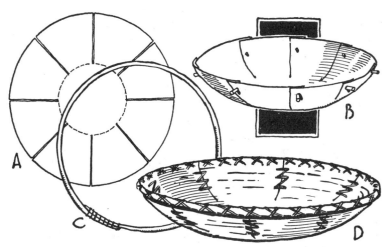

Figure 119. BOWL-SHAPED BASKET OF BIRCH-BARK

The design is applied to the basket with basswood thongs dyed blue and maroon.

Bowl-Shaped Baskets.—Here is a circular basket that is a marked departure from the style described thus far, but it is no oddity in the basket line, nor is it a newcomer, for it has served as a food bowl among the Woodland Indians these countless years. And today it is a favorite as a sewing basket.

Cut out a circular piece of bark sixteen inches in diameter, and draw a circle with a compass in the center of it eight-and-one-half inches across, as shown in A, Figure 119. Make this circle smaller if you want a deeper basket, and larger for a more shallow one. Cut eight slits from the edge of the bark inward to the circle, as in A. Now bend up these eight sections so that the edges overlap one inch at the top; punch a hole through the two layers of bark at each over-lapping, and hold temporarily with wooden pegs as in B. Fit the round hoop around the top and lash the bark firmly to it in the usual manner. Then withdraw the pegs and lace up the sides as in D, Figure 119.

Temporary and Emergency Baskets.—In the life of the far woods it frequently becomes necessary to put together a basket quickly for emergency use, with no thought of keeping it permanently. This was more or less of a routine occurrence to the Woodland Indians on the long treks into remote country, for needless to say these roamers of the woods had little fancy for hauling equipment when the generous wilds were on every hand.

In A, Figure 120, we have a temporary basket which can be made in a few minutes from a single sheet of bark, and which can be used for serving hot dishes since it is waterproof, there being no apertures. A thin piece of bark is needed, which is folded up at the sides and ends with the corners arranged as illustrated. There are two methods of fastening the corners, both suggested in A, Figure 120: a twig may be split and slipped over the bark, or a hole may be punched through the two layers of bark through which a strand of basswood bark is passed and tied.

Another basket of quick construction is shown in E, Figure 120; but this one requires lacing and hence takes a little longer. The end sections of the pattern in D are folded up, the end extensions of the sides bent around outside, and the seams laced without the use of a hoop at the top.

Wash-Basin, Liquid Bowl, or Sap Trough.—The baskets shown in B and C, Figure 120 are frequently regarded as temporary or emer-gency baskets because of their quick construction, but they are quite substantial and make excellent camp wash-basins or liquid containers. Thin birch-bark is gathered at the ends in several overlapping folds and tied at the ends as in the illustration, giving the basket somewhat the appearance of a canoe. Better than birch-bark for this particular type of wash-basin is the bark of cottonwood, basswood, elm, or poplar, but these rough barks must be thinned at the ends before the folding will be possible, removing the woody outer bark and leaving the full thickness only in the main body of the basket—C in Figure 120 illustrates such a basket.

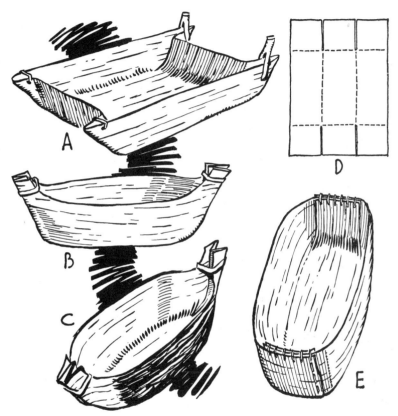

Figure 120. TEMPORARY AND EMERGENCY BARK BASKETS

BASKETS MADE OF MORE THAN ONE PIECE OF BARK

The taste of the white man has placed a premium upon round birch-bark baskets of the general shape of the flower-pot and the waste-basket, and while this shape was not unknown in the old days, certain it is that the Chippewa craftsmen have given themselves to this style in recent years to an extent unknown to their fathers. A basket of this type requires the use of more than one piece of bark and so their making presents a bit more of a problem than those described in the preceding section.

Waste-Paper Baskets.—The most popular of all birch-bark projects today are the beautiful, light, durable scrap-baskets. Beside me as I write is such a basket, twenty-four inches in height and eighteen inches in diameter, an ornament for any office, with ten years of use behind it and promising a lifetime of service in the future. Such waste-baskets are the proper thing for a camp headquarters, a resort, or a den in the city.

Much of the attractiveness of the waste-basket depends on the beauty of the birch-bark, and consequently pains should be taken to select a sheet of thick, heavy bark, smooth and free from blemishes, and of delightful color. These big baskets call for particularly heavy bark. Since the best baskets are made from a single sheet of bark taken from a large tree, the width of the basket usually depends on the width of the tree. The best baskets are about fifteen inches in width, and range in height from eighteen to twenty-two inches.

If sheets of bark in these large sizes are not available, smaller dimensions are of course possible or the basket may be made from two sheets of bark, laced together down each side of the basket, as described later for the small round baskets (the pattern shown in A, Figure 123 will be just right if the dimensions are increased so as to make a basket of the desired size).

Figure 121 illustrates the waste-basket we shall describe in detail, made of one large sheet of bark. In A we have an untapered basket, as wide at the bottom as at the top—these are more attractive than the tapered ones and certainly are easier to make. Keeping the brown side out, curl the bark around, allowing an overlapping of at least an inch and a half, and hold it in place temporarily with two or three wooden pegs. Make two strong wooden hoops of exactly the same size, as nearly circular as possible, and attach one at the top and the other at the bottom by tying temporarily. Lace up the side of the basket with uncolored basswood-bark thongs, as shown in A—note that the lacings overlap each other slightly. Now lace the hoops, top and bottom, firmly in place with the style of lacing shown in C, Figure 121. Colored bark lacings in red, blue, or green should be used to hold the top hoop, but not for the side of the basket.

With the top and bottom hoops laced permanently, cut out a circular piece of very heavy bark for the bottom, made just the right

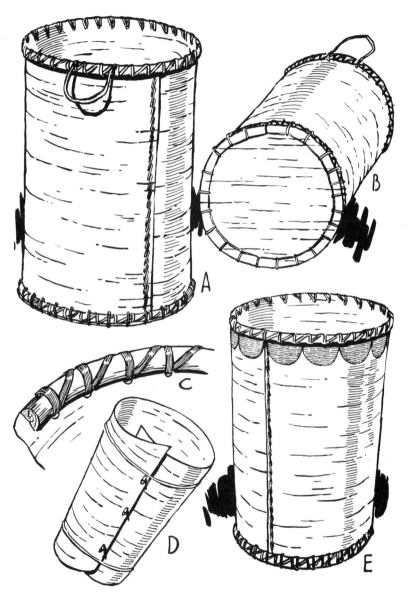

Figure 121. WASTE-BASKETS OF BIRCH-BARK

size by placing the basket on the bark and tracing around it. Tie the bottom in place temporarily and then lace it on firmly as shown in B, Figure 121: the thong goes around the hoop and through the bark of both the sides and bottom, and is half-hitched on the bottom of each hole, as indicated in B. The basswood-bark lacings must be well soaked and kept wet while using. A handle may be attached to the hoop at the top, as seen in A, made by twisting together four thongs of basswood bark.

A decoration often used on this type of basket by Indian basket-makers is shown at the top of the basket in E, Figure 121. It is made by cutting a three-inch strip of bark into the scalloped design illustrated, and dyeing it with blue, red, or green dye. When the basket is being constructed, this strip is inserted at the top, over the side bark and under the top hoop, and held in place by the hoop lacings.

If a tapered waste-basket is preferred (E, Figure 121), curl the rectangular sheet of bark and adjust until it has the taper desired, then peg the sides temporarily as illustrated in D. Put on the top and bottom hoops, being sure they are parallel to each other, and tie in place temporarily. Then with the tin-shears, cut off the excess bark along the hoops at the top and bottom. Draw a perpendicular line down the side as a guide for the side lacing, and when this lacing is completed, cut off the excess bark with the tin-shears. Complete the basket as described above.

Small Round Baskets.—Small round baskets present a more pleasing appearance if they are tapered, that is, if the top is a little larger than the bottom. This is best accomplished if the sides are made in four sections laced together. If perpendicular sides are acceptable, all that is needed is to coil a piece of bark of the proper size and lace the edges together.

Figure 122 shows a very attractive round basket with slanting sides. The pattern of the side pieces is shown in A. Cut to the dimensions indicated, the basket will have a top diameter of about twelve inches, a bottom diameter of nine inches, and a height of six inches.

Four pieces will be needed of the size and shape indicated in the pattern. Overlap the edges of these a half inch, and punch two holes through the two layers at each overlapping, and insert wooden pegs to hold the basket in shape temporarily. Now put the hoops around the top and bottom and tie temporarily in four or five places in the usual manner, and then lace up the side seams with uncolored basswood thongs so that they appear as in the drawing of the finished basket.

Next a circular piece of bark must be cut for the bottom, this being accomplished by placing the basket on the bark, running a pencil around the lower hoop, and cutting the bark accordingly. Place the bottom in position and tie it temporarily to the hoop in two or three places. Holes should now be punched along the bottom hoop

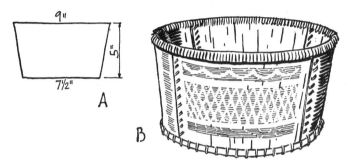

Figure 122. A Round Birch-bark Basket with Scraped Design

both above it through the sides and below it through the bottom; the laces should then be run through these holes binding both the hoop and the bottom in place. With the bottom laced, complete the basket by binding the top hoop permanently in place using either of the styles of lacing shown in B and D, Figure 113, preferably the latter.

The sides of the basket should be made with the brown side of the bark to the outside, but the bottom piece should be placed with the brown side toward the *inside* of the basket.

Baskets of the Flower-Pot Type.—To call it a flower-pot is to place undue limitations on the pleasing basket shown in Figure 123, but among the many appropriate uses to which it can be put, certainly we must not omit its contribution to the flower window in the sun-room. And in respect to flower-pots, let it be known that birch-bark is no misfit, for no flower that grows ever radiated its sunshine of beauty from a more completely appropriate setting. The bark blends with the plant and seems somehow to belong.

Now to the making: The basket is in no wise different from the round basket just described except that its sides are made from three pieces of bark each cut to the size and shape set forth in B, Figure 123. Using this layout, proceed as before and the result will be a basket six-and-one-half inches in diameter at the top and five-and-one-half

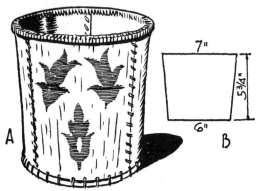

Figure 123. A Basket of the Flower-pot Type with Scraped Floral Designs

at the bottom. Change the dimensions as desired for larger and smaller pots. Remember that the brown side of the bark should be up in the bottom piece, and out in the side pieces.

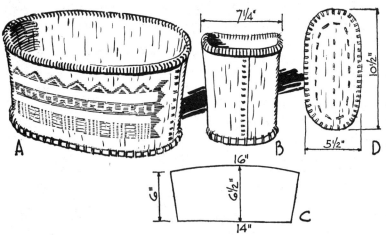

Figure 124. An Oblong Basket with Scraped Design

It is possible to make tapered round baskets from a single piece of bark by coiling it as in making the tapered waste-basket shown in D,

Figure 121, and described on page 52. Better results are obtained in small baskets, however, if the sides are made from three or four pieces as in the two just described.

An Oblong Basket.—Mother is certain to lay claim to this basket for if she does not need it as a sewing basket she will have visions of it harboring twin plants or a trailing vine in the solarium. It is an oblong basket with slightly sloping sides made of two pieces of bark as shown in Figure 124. The pattern for the side pieces is shown in C and the bottom in D. Proceed with the making just as in the case of the small round baskets just described. Note in D that the bottom has a decoration made by a thong of basswood bark run through holes punched in it.

Decorating Birch-Bark Baskets

Birch-bark itself is so beautiful and decorative that to add elaborate ornamentation to a basket is like placing a painting in an over-tinseled frame. There are a few devices for ornamentation employed by the Woodland Indians, however, most of which have already been discussed, that are entirely appropriate and in keeping with the tone of the baskets: (1) borders of basswood-bark lacings, (2) overlaid borders of birch-bark, (3) designs created on the birch-bark with yarn or basswood-bark strands, (4) scraped designs. Porcupine quills are seldom used on baskets but are common and appropriate decorations for boxes.

The use of borders of basswood-bark lacings both plain and colored have been discussed amply in the preceding pages—the binding of the hoop to the top of a basket creates a border that may be made decorative by using one of the stitches shown in Figure 113. Overlaid borders of birch-bark have also been referred to and are seen in Figures 121 and 136, the former being of dyed bark. Designs applied with colored yarn are used only on small objects such as napkin-rings and are discussed in the early pages of this chapter. Basswood-bark strands may be effectively employed to create designs on the sides of baskets if care is taken to select smooth strands of uniform width—such designs are seen in Figures 116 and 118.

Scraped Designs on Birch-Bark.—Here is by all odds the most appropriate method of ornamentation for birch-bark, and probably the most ancient for it appears on very old baskets from many northern and eastern woodland tribes. It consists of creating designs by scraping off a very thin layer of the brown bark, exposing the lighter brown of the under layer. Such a treatment is seen in Figures 122, 123, and 124.

Not all bark is suitable for this type of treatment in that the bark varies greatly in the depth of the brown on its inner or trunk side.

Figure 125. CHIPPEWA GEOMETRIC DESIGNS FOR USE ON BASKETS

Select bark that has as dark a brown on its inner side as can be found and make the basket as usual with the brown side out. Draw the design on the basket with a pencil, and then trace the lines with a pointed instrument, creasing the bark slightly; or better still, cut the design out of cardboard, place it on the bark and run a pointed instrument around it. Now scrape the bark with the blade of a small jackknife, beginning at the edge of the design and working away from it. The dark tan surface consists of a very thin layer that scales off easily under the knife, and beneath it is a lighter shade of tan that blends with it delightfully. The scraping completed, the design stands out vividly in the darker tan. The slight crease made by the pointed instrument prevents the knife from slipping accidentally across the edge of the pattern. Of course the colors can be reversed if desired, and the design itself scraped to the lighter shade, leaving the main areas of the basket dark, but the usual procedure is as described.

Now to the question of appropriate designs: These are Woods Indian baskets and should be decorated in the true and ancient fashion of the woodlands, avoiding all modern or "civilized" contributions. Here as in all efforts at Indian art the best results are obtained by

Figure 126. CHIPPEWA FLORAL DESIGNS FOR BASKETS

adhering strictly to original Indian motifs and not attempting to improvise. Two types of design are characteristic of Chippewa and other Woodland baskets—the geometric or line patterns such as are seen on the baskets in Figure 122, and the floral figures of the type in Figure 117. Both are ancient and traditional types although the conventional floral designs of long years past that suggest flowers and leaves underwent an evolution during the middle of the last century until today more realistic patterns appear that are unquestionably an imitation of nature and therefore of less artistic merit than their symbolic predecessors. The ancient conventional patterns still appear in generous quantities, however.

Suitable geometric patterns for baskets are seen in Figures 122, 124, and 125. The baskets in Figures 117 and 123 offer designs of the conventional floral type and others are suggested in Figure 126, all ancient Chippewa patterns. These should be cut out of cardboard

and the various cards arranged on the basket in various combinations
until a satisfying grouping is found.

WATERPROOF BARK KETTLES AND UTENSILS

The bark of the white birch supplied not only the baskets of the
Red Indians of the northern and eastern woodlands, but also the
water buckets and cooking kettles! Cook in inflammable birch-bark?
Certainly—but first let us make the kettles!

Kettles are made waterproof by sealing the seams with a mixture
made from the gum or pitch of evergreen trees. In addition to their
permanent kettles made in this way, the Chippewas made temporary
or emergency kettles of one uncut piece of bark which had no seams
to seal. Let us consider these temporary kettles first, and then the
permanent ones.

Temporary or Emergency Kettles

Earlier in this chapter we discussed a temporary or emergency
basket or tray which is waterproof in that it is made of an uncut sheet

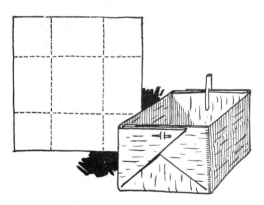

Figure 127. A Temporary or Emergency Waterproof Kettle

of bark—this is pictured in A, Figure 120. Such a tray may serve as a
liquid container but it will scarcely do as a kettle.

In Figure 127, however, we have an excellent temporary cooking
kettle of thin birch-bark. From the dotted lines on the pattern and the
picture of the finished basket, the method of construction is clearly
understandable—fasten the ends either by a split stick or a thong of

basswood bark, both of which are shown in the drawing., Such a kettle can be made in ten minutes without worry about pine pitch for the seams since none exist.

MAKING A PITCH-SEALED KETTLE.

Figure 128 shows the ideal type of construction for a kettle or bucket that is to hold liquids. It is to be preferred to the square and rectangular baskets of the early pages of this chapter, because the seams, consisting of half-inch overlapping of bark, are more easily sealed than baskets with double layers of bark at the ends. This is an

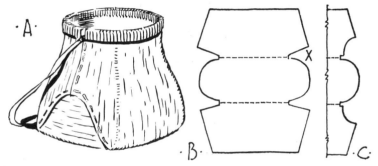

Figure 128. IDEAL CONSTRUCTION FOR A BASKET TO BE WATERPROOFED FOR USE AS A KETTLE

ancient style of construction among the Chippewas for both baskets and kettles, but being a little more difficult to fashion it is seldom employed today unless the container is to be waterproofed.

The layout is shown in B, Figure 128; this pattern should be carefully cut from cardboard and then traced on the bark. The three sections indicated by the dotted lines are of equal size. The slits at X are about one-third the height of the sides of the basket. Having cut the bark to this shape, fold up the sides on the dotted lines, then fold up the curved end pieces and bend the end extensions of the sides around outside the curved ends. Punch holes through these square end sections where they overlap and fasten temporarily with wooden pegs. Now with a pencil mark the outline of the curved end sections on the bark beneath them and cut this bark a half inch below the line thus drawn, in order that there will be a half-inch overlapping. When this is done the ends of the pattern will appear as in C.

With the basket held together temporarily by wooden pegs, place the hoop in place at the top and tie it temporarily. As the basket sits on the table be sure that the hoop is parallel to the surface of the table, and then trim off the excess bark even with the top of the hoop. Now lace the hoop permanently in place and lace up the end seams in the usual way. The ends of the finished basket should appear as in A.

The basket is now complete and ready to be waterproofed.

MAKING THE PITCH FOR WATERPROOFING

The *bigiu* or pitch so essential for waterproofing baskets, mending leaks in canoes, and fashioning torches for hunting, is made from the gum that oozes from the trunks of evergreen trees. To one who is not searching for it, this pitch is one of the nuisances of the woods that is forever getting into his hair and on his hands and clothing, and gumming up his ax handles, but once he goes on the hunt for it, he finds it a rare item indeed to locate in sufficient quantities. The reason rests in the fact that the gum oozes through the bark in lumps large enough to see only where the bark has been severed. It can be produced easily merely by scraping the bark of an evergreen tree and then waiting a day or two for the gum to ooze out. The Chippewas in the old days would go into the woods in the summer and scrape the bark of many trees, and then return later to harvest the gum in quantities sufficient to last for many months to come. The gum can be scraped from the tree with a knife or stick and placed in a container. One evergreen tree is as good as another so far as variety goes, but the old Chippewas say that *the best gum comes from trees growing in a swamp or near the water's edge.*

The crude gum as gathered must now be placed in a kettle of water and boiled, which causes the pure gum to rise to the surface so that it can be skimmed off. The crude gum of course contains bark and other debris and much of this will also rise to the surface, making it difficult to skim the gum cleanly. The Chippewas put the gum as they gathered it into a loosely woven bag made of strips of basswood-bark and would throw this bag into the kettle—the gum would escape through the holes in the bag but the other debris would not. If only a little gum is needed it can doubtless be skimmed off without the use of a bag, but if much is desired, the gum should be placed in a coarsely woven sack such as those in which onions are sold, and this bag placed in the kettle.

As the gum is skimmed, it should be placed in a container and saved until needed, at which time it should be placed in a kettle and heated until it takes on the consistency of a thin paste. Then a small quantity of powdered charcoal should be added and thoroughly mixed through it. The Chippewas used charcoal from white cedar chips, finely powdered, but any powdered charcoal will do. The black gummy mass resulting is now ready for use.

Applying the Pitch.—With the blade of an old knife or a paddle of wood of similar size, apply the black, sticky pitch while it is still hot to the seams of the kettle on the outside, working it well into the crevices between the bark, into the holes and over the lacings. Apply it generously to the seams but be careful not to smear it over a wider area than necessary. The finished kettle should show clean black lines about a half inch wide along the seams. Allow the pitch to set for a little while and then test the kettle by filling it with water. When the leaks are discovered apply a little more pitch to them.

Repairing Leaks in Birch-bark Canoes.—Leaks in birch-bark canoes are repaired by filling the cracks with pitch by the method just described.

Using Paper and Bark Kettles on the Fire

Birch-bark is one of the most inflammable materials to be found and is the universal tinder of the Northwoods, so combustible that it will burn lustily in the rain—can it then be used as a cooking kettle on the fire? Yes, and it can be placed right in the flames! just as can paper that has been shaped into a kettle! *The trick is in so arranging the kettle on the campfire that the flames do not touch the basket above the water line.* The water on the inside prevents the bark from burning, but if the actual flames come in contact with the bark above the level of the water, it will surely ignite.

If you do not believe that this can be done, try it out by folding a piece of paper into a container and placing it on the gas stove in the kitchen. Use ordinary wrapping paper or even a sheet of typewriter paper. Fold it into a kettle as indicated in Figure 127 and fasten the ends with paper-clips. Fill with water, place on the gas stove and turn the flames up as high as you choose—the water will soon be boiling and the paper not even scorched.

So when you are in the birch country, you need never want for a vessel in which to boil water or cook food.

Bark Dippers, Cups and Saucers

The old-time Chippewas sometimes made watertight eating bowls and saucers from birch-bark but for the most part they relied on large shells and other objects for these and used bark dishes only for dry foods. Bowls of the size of breakfast-food bowls can be made by

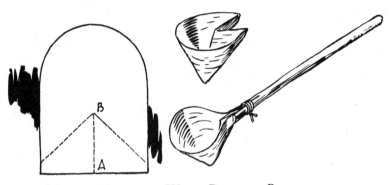

Figure 129. Water Dipper of Bark

using the pattern for the round bowl shown in Figure 119, but making it with four instead of eight slits and omitting the hoop at the top. The seams should then be well sealed with pitch.

In Figure 129, we have a type of water dipper suggested by Horace Kephart. Cut the bark as shown, crease along the dotted lines with a pointed instrument, and fold to shape; then insert in the split stick and tie as indicated.

A tumbler can be fashioned of bark by coiling a sheet for the sides and lacing the ends together, then sewing a circular bottom in place, all seams to be made watertight with pitch.

BARK BOXES

Boxes can be made in a great variety of shapes and sizes, two or three samples of which will suffice to indicate the methods of construction.

A Food Box for the Trail

Here is a little box in which to carry food on the trail, particularly useful for greasy stuffs such as butter, lard, bacon, and the like. It packs snugly in any pack and is of a shape to fit the pocket. These boxes were used for many purposes by the Woodland Indians of the North whose life kept them on the trail so much of the year. Bark

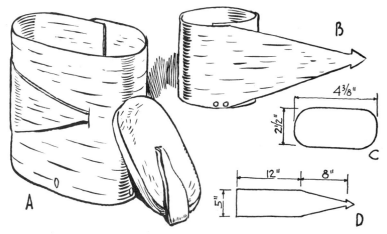

Figure 130. A Food Box of Birch-bark for the Trail

boxes similar to these are said to be used in the woods in northern European countries.

So simple is the box that it can be made in short order. From Figure 130 it will be seen that it is oblong in shape and has a wooden bottom and cover. The bottom and top should be made first, whittled out of half-inch basswood, cedar, or other soft wood—the shape and dimensions are shown in C, Figure 130. Both top and bottom are of exactly the same size and shape, the only difference in the two pieces being that the cover is rounded off on the top side so that the edges are one-fourth inch thick, whereas the bottom remains at full width throughout.

Cut the strip of birch-bark as shown in D. Wrap this around the bottom, beginning with the broad end in the middle of one of the sides of the bottom, and tack with two tacks as shown in B. Continue to wrap the narrow section of bark around the box, and insert the tip into a little slit cut inside the box as shown in A—the shoulders at the end of the strip shown in D will prevent the end from pulling out.

The top is forced down inside the box, and if made exactly the same shape and size as the bottom, will fit very snugly. A handle of buckskin is attached to the middle of the top by forcing both ends of the loop through a small hole and tying, as shown in A—this is essential for withdrawing the top and is also useful in carrying the box.

These boxes may be made of any size but are usually of the size indicated or smaller. They are not watertight, of course, but will carry moist and greasy foods satisfactorily.

Trinket Boxes

The delightful little trinket box shown in A, Figure 131, is about three-and-three-fourths inches in diameter. The sides are made of a strip of smooth medium-thick bark two-and-one-fourth inches wide and twelve-and-one-half inches long, coiled into a circle with the

Figure 131. Trinket Boxes

ends overlapping a quarter inch and sewed together at the seam. Around the inside of the top is sewed a hoop made from a very thin strip of cedar to give support to the box. The cover is three-and-seven-eighths inches in diameter, and five-eighths inches deep, made of two pieces sewed together. A few strands of grass are sewed around the outside of the lower edge of the cover rim, both for stability and ornamentation. In such small boxes, thread is used for sewing the bark together instead of basswood thongs, because the latter is so bulky as to give the box a clumsy appearance.

These little boxes may be decorated with red and blue yarn, or

Figure 132.

better still, with dyed porcupine quills. If quills are used the top of the cover should be made of two layers of bark, the bottom layer serving to protect the ends of the quills which are tucked through holes made in the top layer. The box in B is ornamented with a few quills only, whereas that in A is quilled solidly. When yarn is used,

Figure 133. RECTANGULAR BARK BOX

it should be applied sparingly, merely to create a simple design on the top and sides.

Boxes of this shape may be made in any size desired.

Rectangular Boxes.—Rectangular boxes with covers can be easily made by sewing the sections together with thread. The box shown in

Figure 133, is six inches long, four-and-one-half inches wide and three inches high. The cover must of course be made enough larger to slip over—it is one-and-one-quarter inches deep. Each section of the box and cover is edged with a few strands of fine grass sewed on the outside edge with black thread and then the sections are sewed together into the box.

The box from which this drawing was made was constructed from the bark of wild cherry roots and has much the same tone as birchbark. The decorations are made with white and blue porcupine quills but yarn may be substituted. This box was made many, many years ago by the Indians of Beaver Island in northern Lake Michigan.

MISCELLANEOUS BARK PROJECTS

Now let us consider a number of odds and ends in the line of useful objects that can be made from bark.

Rustic Table Lamps

The woodsy interior of the camp building, country place, or den calls for a rustic table lamp with a bark shade, such as that shown in Figure 134.

Making the Lamp Shade.—Cut out a circular piece of bark and remove a V-shaped section from one side, as shown in A, Figure 134. The width of the V at its widest point should be one-half the diameter of the sheet of bark. That is, if the bark is twenty-four inches in diameter, which is an excellent dimension for a good-sized lamp, the width of the V would be twelve inches.

Curl the sheet into the shape of the shade, overlapping the edges an inch, peg the bark layers together temporarily (B, Figure 134), and then lace the round hoop firmly outside the bark with basswood lacings as in making the bark baskets described earlier in this chapter.

If the shade is used on a commercial table lamp, a hole can be cut at the apex to fit on the lamp standard. However, the effect will be much better if it is used on the rustic lamp described below.

The Lamp Standard.—Select a small white-cedar sapling between two and three inches in diameter which has a sharp curve at the roots similar to that shown in E, Figure 134, white cedar being recommended over other woods merely because the saplings very frequently are curved at the surface of the ground, especially when found in the thick swamps where this tree thrives. Shape the stick as

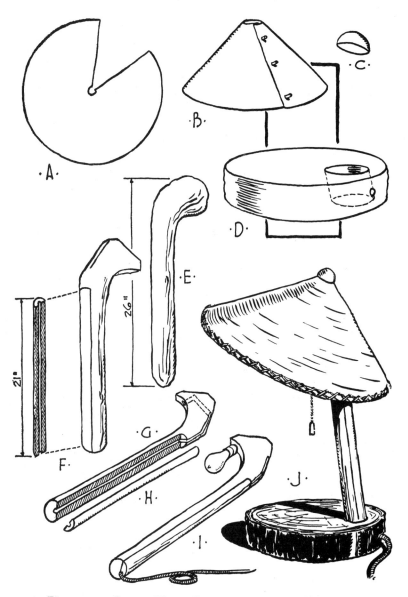

Figure 134. Rustic Table Lamp with Birch-bark Shade

shown in F, Figure 134, and saw off so that it is twenty-six inches
in length over all. Split the stick lengthwise as in G, and cut a groove
throughout the entire length for the lamp cord as shown in H and I.
The horizontal hole, the end of which shows at the top of H, is made
with a brace and bit. Attach the lamp socket as in I, insert the cord,
and nail back the half of the upright which was removed. The base
is made by sawing off a four-inch section of a ten- or eleven-inch log
and boring a slanting hole of the proper size near one side, into which
the upright can be fitted as in the drawing of the finished lamp.

Place the birch-bark lamp shade in position on the lamp, whittle
the semicircular knob of cedar shown in C, three-fourths of an inch
in diameter, place it at the apex of the shade, and nail it to the upright,
thus holding the shade in place.

The groove containing the lamp cord is visible only at the extreme
top of the standard, as can be seen in H and I, but this area is completely covered by the lamp shade.

Figure 135.

INDIAN DANCE RATTLES OF BARK

Gourds provide the favorite dance rattles among the Southwest
Indians, rawhide among the Plains Indians, turtle shells among the
Iroquois, but the ceremonies of the woodland Chippewas are accompanied by the clicking of *birch-bark rattles* in the hands of lusty and
vigorous dancers. B in Figure 135 shows such a rattle.

Cut a rectangular piece of bark seven by twelve inches in size, curl it into a cylinder overlapping the edges three-fourths of an inch, and lace the overlapping bark together. Now whittle two discs from three-eighths-inch cedar or basswood just large enough to fit snugly into the ends, and in the center of each bore a hole a half inch or less in diameter. Next whittle a handle as shown in A, Figure 135, making the slender section just large enough to fit snugly into the holes in the discs.

To assemble the rattle: tack the discs in place at the ends of the bark cylinder with brass-headed tacks, put inside a handful of very small pebbles and a few kernels of corn or wheat, and insert the handle. The handle is held secure by a small peg inserted into a small hole bored through the stick at the top as shown in B. Tie a couple of fluffies or small feathers to a string and attach to the tip of the stick so that the fluffies hang down an inch or two, and the rattle is finished.

WALL MATCH-HOLDER

An excellent and very attractive wall match-holder for kitchen matches is shown in Figure 136—it is designed to hang on the wall beside the kitchen stove or in the den. The pattern illustrated in A should be worked out on cardboard and traced onto the birch-bark. The bark is folded into the shape of the basket as seen in D, held together temporarily with wooden pegs and then laced permanently, following the usual methods of making birch-bark baskets described earlier in this chapter. There are no hoops around the top edges of the basket but rather a double layer of bark is used: The narrow scalloped strip shown in C, three-fourths inch wide, is placed at the top of the lower lip of the basket as can be seen in D and then the two layers of bark bound together with basswood lacings as illustrated. The large scalloped piece shown in B is cut to the same shape as the back of the basket and laced to it around the edges as shown in D. The brown side of the bark is placed out in making the basket and the inserted section shown in B is also placed with the brown side out, thus giving the entire basket a brown appearance. A little loop of basswood bark is inserted between the two layers of bark at the top to provide a nail hanger as illustrated in D. The diamond shaped decoration seen in D is put on with colored basswood-bark lacings.

Table Match-Holders.—The match-holder shown in E, Figure 136, is a very simple project for those whose fingers are accustomed to sewing. The bottom support consists of two layers of thin birch-bark three-and-one-fourth inches in diameter, sewed together. The cup is one-and-one-half inches high, two inches wide at the top, and one-

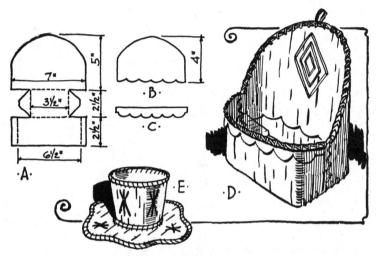

Figure 136. MATCH-HOLDERS

and-one-half inches wide at the bottom. A few strands of grass should be sewed along all the edges of the bark.

PICTURE FRAMES

The attractive rustic picture frames of birch-bark are best made by tacking the bark to a supporting frame of packing-box wood. These frames are favorites for small pictures and photographs, and are made wider than the frames commonly used on small pictures in order to give the bark a chance, two inches being a good width as illustrated in C, Figure 135. Having tacked on the bark, split some one-fourth-inch twigs and edge the bark with them, as in the illustration. The grain of the bark may go crosswise, lengthwise, or diagonally. Oval frames are made by cutting the board to the oval shape with a coping saw and covering with bark.

Bark Coat-Hanger

E in Figure 135 suggests a bark coat-hanger, attractive enough but requiring a great deal of work. The birch-bark section consists of two layers of bark, and the borders are pliable twigs cut in half and wrapped solidly with basswood-bark strands as they are laced to the bark.

Eye Shade or Visor

A serviceable visor may be improvised in the woods by cutting birch-bark to the general pattern used in commercial visors. Two half-inch strips of basswood bark or buckskin are attached to the ends and tied to fit the head. D in Figure 135 shows such a visor.

Arm-Guards for Archery

To make a first-class arm-guard, cut a rectangular piece of birch-bark five inches wide and six or seven inches long, and round off the corners. Shape it to the inside of the forearm and attach a thong of basswood bark or buckskin at each end with which to tie it to the arm.

Figure 137.

Bark Archery Quivers.—Figure 137 shows the method of making a quiver for the carrying of arrows. It is four or five inches in diameter and about twenty inches long. The shoulder strap is made of an inch strip of basswood bark. The cover illustrated is not used when the container is to be used for arrows.

Headdress Carrier.—A case for a war-bonnet after the manner of the parfleche ones used by the Plains Indians may be made from birch-bark, constructed exactly like the archery quiver and shown in Figure 137. It should be six to eight inches in diameter and twenty-seven inches long, with cover attached as illustrated.

Window Boxes for Flowers

In making a window box for flowers, a framework of wooden strips should be built, on which the heavy bark is to be tacked. When the bark is in place, twigs or sticks a half inch in diameter should be split in half and tacked along the edges—it is never satisfactory to tack the bark without the additional support of the split sticks.

Writing Paper

Very thin birch-bark is the writing paper of the woods, light, flat, thin, waterproof, and sweetly scented. No one could ask for a more appropriate or beautiful paper on which to convey the loveliest of thoughts.

Note Books

A number of thin sheets of bark of the thickness of writing paper can be bound together into a little note book by using heavier bark for the covers. Edge the covers with sweet grass or a strip from a cattail leaf sewed on with black thread, as described under the discussion of napkin-rings. Sew the book together with thread. Decorate

Figure 138. Note book of Birch-bark

the cover with colored yarn or porcupine quills. Figure 138 shows such a booklet measuring four by six inches in size and containing thirty-six sheets of bark paper.

Book Covers.—Heavy birch-bark makes excellent covers for camp logs, memory books, camp picture albums, campers' address books, note books and the like. The bark should measure an inch larger than the paper it covers, and should be edged on all sides with sweet grass or cattail leaves sewed with thread. Punch holes through the bark and paper and tie into a book with buckskin thongs. The inner or brown side of the bark should be used for the outside of the cover.

Such a book can be lettered or decorated with designs by scraping the bark as described under the section of this chapter entitled "Decorating Birch-Bark Baskets."

WOODCRAFT ROPE AND CORDAGE

STORY COMING DOWN from early pioneer days has it that two Indians, made drunk by a trader's liquor while being relieved of their furs, were tossed into their canoe in a stupor and shoved out into the Niagara River. When they awoke they found themselves on Goat Island between the Canadian and American Falls, to which some guardian angel must have guided them, for had they skirted its edge with the roaring current the awful doom of the Falls would surely have been theirs. But even as it was, it seemed to the ever-growing crowd of spectators that death by starvation was their inevitable lot for the island was surrounded on three sides by seething rapids and falls, and on the fourth by the steep precipitous drop of the cliff. Defeat was not that easily accepted, however, for woodsmen as they were, they promptly made a rope of basswood bark found on the island with which they lowered themselves over the cliff to freedom.

Time will come and soon, if we get far enough back in the wilds so that the corner store is out of hailing distance, when we will need string and rope—for cordage is an item that comes close to being an essential in the woods, where it does the usual duties of rope and string plus the customary function of nails. Nails the bush will not produce (except for those uses where wooden pegs will suffice) but rope and string is there aplenty, no matter what part of the country one is in, and from materials the average person knows and can recognize without the advice of a naturalist.

There are two chief sources of cordage in the woods, the bark

74

and roots of trees, and the hide, sinew and hair of animals. The timber folk, both red and white, use the former nine times out of ten.

Bark Cordage

Perhaps you need a fish stringer, perchance a lashing to hold together the frame of a lean-to, or a strap for your pack, or a temporary rope for the tent. For such uses the *whole bark* just as it is ripped from the tree will fill the bill without the fuss and bother of separating the layers and turning the strands into rope. Just peel loose a strip and proceed with the lashing. Here are the trees whose bark will not fail you: *slippery elm, young basswood or linden, pawpaw, young hickory,* and *leatherwood.* Remove the bark vertically from up the side of the tree—make a two-inch cut near the ground, grasp the bark and rip it loose; it will become narrower and narrower and finally free itself far above your head, thus producing a long useful strip.

Small Cordage and String

Basswood or *linden* bark is synonomous with cordage in the woods. It is the bast or inner bark that possesses strength, the rough outer bark contributing nothing and it is left on in the coarse lashings in the preceding paragraph only to save the inconvenience of removing it. The inner bark of basswood or linden is exceedingly strong; in fact, the term *bast rope*, while actually referring to cordage from the inner bark of any tree, usually is thought of in woods parlance as meaning basswood rope, so completely have these strong fibers become associated with cordage. This is the *wigub* of the Indians. There is no finer source of string, rope, or vegetable thongs in the woods. Nor is there any bark so easy to prepare into cordage.

If basswood is available there is no need of looking farther, but in case the woods do not offer it, the following barks all make good cordage: *elm*—particularly *slippery, American* or *white,* and *wahoo* or *winged,* the *hickories, white oak, red cedar, cypress, pawpaw, Osage-orange, leatherwood,* and *black locust.* Of these elm is probably the most commonly used.

The basswood bark should be stripped, soaked for ten days, the inner bark separated from the outer, and then separated into narrow strands *as described in complete and ample detail on pages 28 to 30 in Chapter X on "Bark-craft."* No further details regarding the process are needed here.

These narrow strands of bast measuring an eighth to a quarter of an inch in width make good lacings just as they stand, entirely suitable for average uses without the necessity of turning them into round cordage. When well soaked they are pliable, smooth, slippery, and take a knot reasonably well, but when dry are too stiff to handle. A supply should be kept in water constantly when they are apt to be needed.

The time will come, however, when we will need round twine as soft and pliable when dry as when wet, which can be picked up and used without soaking. Here is how it is made: Put a good quantity of ashes from the campfire into a kettle and boil for ten minutes, then drain off the water containing the lye of the ashes into another kettle. Into this put a good wide strip of basswood or other inner bark and place on the campfire, there to boil off and on for twenty-four hours—constant boiling is unnecessary but just when the campfire is going for cooking or other purposes. Now put the bark strips around a smooth pole (the Indians use the shoulder blade of a deer) and, taking one end in each hand, pull back and forth until the fine threads begin to separate one from another. The fiber is now ready to be turned into string or rope.

To make the twine, separate from the hank two thin strands as long as can be secured, lay them over the thigh and roll the palm of the right hand over them in one direction, twisting them together into a round twine. Pull the twine across the thigh with the left hand as each section is finished and continue the rolling until the ends of the strands are neared. Cut off the end of one of the strands so that the two are of unequal length by about six inches, then lay in a new strand at the end of the short one and continue the rolling. When the end of the second or longer strand is reached, splice on another in the same way, continuing until the cord is as long as desired. The squaw of the Indian village of the northern woods will turn out twine in this way with remarkable rapidity.

Making Bark Rope

I have seen basswood rope in the Chippewa villages that seemed superior in every way to the commercial Manila rope we use today, much lighter in weight, smoother, silky to the touch, easier to handle, being free from the slivers or "whiskers" that cut and burn the skin, less inclined to kink, and smooth and oily to the touch when wet. I once saw an old Indian make a hundred feet of as fine half-inch rope as one could hope to see, which he planned to use to support his fishnet in the lake, but a couple of days later when again I visited him, the old fellow's spirit was crushed—some white fishermen had come along and cut the rope, dragged it with them a space and let it sink, net and all, their obvious purpose being to rid the lake of net fishing, yet the Indian was obviously within his reservation rights.

Slippery elm also makes a fine rope and any of the barks listed on page 75 may be used, although basswood is usually preferred if obtainable.

The inner bark is prepared by boiling in lye water made from ashes and rubbed as described in the preceding section. A large quantity will be needed, and the shredded barks should be kept in water until used.

Separate a long strand having half the thickness of the rope desired, and hang it over a nail driven in a tree. The two ends should be of unequal length as they hang, one at least a foot

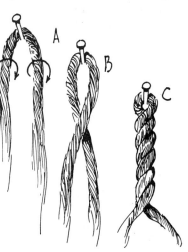

Figure 139. MAKING ROPE OF BASSWOOD BARK

longer than the other. Take one strand in each hand just below the nail; with the fingers twist the strands from left to right and then lay the strand in the right hand over the one in the left and change hands —see Figure 139. Then repeat the process: twist hard as before and lay the right strand over the left. In other words, the separate strands are twisted in one direction and then the two strands are twisted together in the opposite direction. Keep this up and you will soon have rope. When you take it off the nail and let go, it will not unwind. When you reach the end of the short strand, lay in another strand of equal size and proceed as before. And whenever one strand becomes too thin, just lay in another strand to bring it up to size. Be sure to keep the bast wet while working, and when you lay the rope aside for a rest, place it in water.

When the rope is of the desired length it must be stretched and dried. Select two saplings about half the length of the rope apart, tie one end securely to one sapling, pass the rope around the other and pull it as tightly as possible, tying the end to the first sapling. At intervals of three or four times a day untie and stretch again, taking up the slack. In about forty-eight hours, or when the rope seems thoroughly dry, remove it and trim and smooth it up with a knife and scissors, clipping off all the projecting tufts, at the points where the new strands were laid in, and all protruding whiskers. The result should be a strong, smooth rope, soft to the touch.

Making a Lariat

I have a forty-foot lariat which I made of basswood bark by the method just described. It is as fine a practical rope as one could want—certainly it is easier on the hands than other types of rope and is less affected by moisture. Its one shortcoming as a catch-rope is its lightness, for when a rope does not have sufficient weight it will not carry to its mark on long throws.

To turn a rope into a lariat, all that is needed is to make a honda on one end. There are many methods of doing this but the easiest

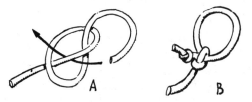

Figure 140. The Lariat Loop

and quickest is to tie a lariat loop. Simply tie an overhand knot about ten inches from one end, leaving the knot open as in A, Figure 140. Then insert the end through the knot following the course of the arrow in A. Tie an overhand knot in this end as illustrated to prevent it from pulling through and jam the whole knot tightly. The finished job appears as in B, the diameter of the loop being about two-and-one-half inches. The lariat loop makes a nicely shaped honda, producing a round loop that stays open all the time, and the weight of the knot is sufficient to facilitate throwing.

ROOT CORDAGE

Probably next in popularity to the *wigub* or cordage of basswood bark, among the red timber folk, are the *wadub* or lacings of split spruce roots. Remarkably tough and strong are these rootlets of the *white spruce*, and pliable enough so that one can tie them into knots as readily as he ties his boot strings.

Other rootlets that find use as cordage are *tamarack, cedar, fir, hemlock, cottonwood, long-leaf pine,* and *digger pine.*

Very slender rootlets of spruce or the other trees may be dug up that when barked will be of the usual size of twine—these are ready for use when soaked in hot water, barked, and scrubbed clean. A quantity may be gathered and put away until needed, when they should be well soaked to render them pliable. Lye water made by boiling ashes in water for ten minutes always does much to soften root and bark cordage, but if the rootlets are to be used as they are and not turned into twisted twine, its use will scarcely be necessary. If the rootlets are to be used immediately after they are dug up, an easy way to prepare them is to bury them for an hour or so in hot ashes, there to let them steam and soften.

Large rootlets of the size of a large quill up to that of a pencil, after being barked and scrubbed clean, should be split in half, or if large enough, quartered, to produce strings of the size desired.

Now these rootlets, either whole or split, will make acceptable string just as they are if only short lengths are needed—they were so used by the Indians for lacing birch-bark baskets, pots, canoes, and the like. If long string is needed, the rootlets should be boiled in lye water and rolled over the thigh into a twisted cord just as described earlier in this chapter for making bark string.

Root cordage may be dyed to any color as described for dyeing lacings in Chapter X, "Bark-craft."

TWINE MADE FROM HERBS

Along with their *wigub* and *wadub*, the Chippewas made extensive use of *zesub* or cord made from nettle-stalk fiber. The stalks of the nettle (*Urticastrum divaricatum*) are best for the purpose in the fall when they have dried in the field but may be used green. The very fine, strong twine from this plant was the favorite material for the fishnets of the early days and many such nets are still made and used. In making the twine the fibrous stalks are treated in exactly the same way as is the basswood bark already described, and the finished product is said to be more than fifty times stronger than twine of similar size made of cotton.

Another source of cordage among the Chippewas is the outer covering of bulrushes (*Scirpus vilidus*). This is a little difficult to secure because the outer layer loosens and falls under the water, remaining attached at the roots. The strands are twisted into twine as in making basswood cordage and two of these twines are then twisted together if larger cord or rope is desired.

String of unusually fine quality is also made from swamp milkweed (*Asclepias incarnata*) and from Indian hemp (*Apocynum cannabinum*). Soak the stems until the whole bark can be removed easily and then scrub off the outer bark leaving the fibrous bast or inner layer. This can be stripped up and used as it is, or can be worked until the threads begin to separate and then twisted into twine by the methods already described for bark string.

Withes—The Wire of the Wilds

A withe is made by twisting a green shoot until the fibers begin to loosen, thus making it pliable. It is used where great strength is needed, where toughness is essential because of the battering it will receive. Withes were used to make the hinges for doors and gates in pioneer days, to "wire" together the logs of a raft.

Hickory is the first choice because of its great strength and toughness, and because its fibers quickly loosen and become pliable—for heavy duty go out of your way to find it. But these will all serve admirably: *white oak, black ash, birches, wild raisin* or *withe-rod, willow, sweet gum, witch-hazel* and *chestnut.*

To make the withe, select a tall shoot and without cutting it grasp it in the hands at the end and twist it. Keep twisting and pulling, putting on the pressure until its fibers loosen and separate into strands. The withe will then be pliable and can be bent and tied. It is usually possible for a strong-handed man to twist a shoot considerably larger than his thumb, although withes of that size are seldom needed. If the fibers refuse to loosen under the twisting, cut the branch or shoot, lay it across a log and pound it thoroughly with a wooden maul on all sides and from end to end; then place your foot on one end and twist. Remember that young shoots are stronger always than branches cut from a grown tree.

Withes are tied by means of the *binder knot*, executed by twisting the ends around each other twice—the ends are not doubled back against themselves, but merely twisted around each other. This is the simplest knot known but will not slip, and is the only one usable for the more or less stiff withes.

Withe Whip or Quirt.—A first-class riding quirt or a short bull whip can be made from a *hickory* or *white oak* withe. Select a shoot of the size of a broomstick and as tall as can be found. Twist it thoroughly before cutting it, and when as loose and flexible as it can be made, cut it and pound it with a maul to further loosen the fibers, working over its entire length save six inches at the butt end which is to be the handle. Separate the loose strands and pound the core or heart if need be. Then divide the strands into four equal strips and plait them into the whip, cutting out some of the strands with every few inches as the work progresses in order to give the whip the usual taper. Make a six-inch cracker for the tip from swamp milkweed (page 262) and you will have a serviceable lash entirely from woodsy materials.*

Cordage from Hide, Hair and Sinew

For tying small bundles the Indians frequently used strips of buckskin or rawhide. The latter applied wet will shrink as it dries and bind with exceeding tightness.

Rawhide Rope.—The Plains Indians frequently made long rope of rawhide, the lariats of the early West being an example of the excellence of such cordage. These are a little difficult to fashion because of the round, strong core that forms the center, unless one has a cotton line to use for the purpose. Minus this, a strip of rawhide would have to be rolled into a round core. Now four rawhide thongs are needed one-third longer than the length of the rope desired and of such size that the width of all four equals the circumference of the core. These long thongs are made by going round and round a hide with scissors, stripping it into the long strand. Buffalo, buck, and elk

---

* For a discussion of whip cracking, and of making leather whips and crackers, see Bernard S. Mason, *Primitive and Pioneer Sports* (New York: A. S. Barnes and Company, 1937).

were used in the early days. Attach the core to a spike driven in a pole, tie the four strands to the core just below the spike, and plait the four thongs over the core. The rawhide must be kept wet throughout. When finished the wet rope should be placed in a kettle of warm, melted animal tallow and left until the tallow has permeated the rawhide thoroughly, the temperature being kept nearly constant throughout. Remove the rope, let it stand for a few hours to set the tallow, then work back and forth around a pole to limber and loosen.

Sinew Thread.—The almost universal thread among the Indians was sinew or strands from the tendons of the buffalo, deer, or beef, usually taken from along the backbone. When soaked these large tendons can be separated into strands of the size of thread which are exceedingly strong. Even today the Plains Indians look askance at any beaded work made with modern thread, regarding sinew as essential to good workmanship.

Hair Rope.—In the West and Southwest hair from horses' manes and tails was a commonly used material for ropes in the early days, riatas of this type being no rarity in the southwest states and Mexico even to this day. The Woodland Indians seldom practiced this art although they did make beautiful roaches or head ornaments from the hair of deer and of porcupine combined.

To make a hair rope, take a pinch of horsehair in the fingers, hang it over a nail driven in a post, and proceed to twist it into twine using the method described for making bark rope on page 77 and illustreated in Figure 139. The cord thus produced should be one-fourth the size of the desired rope. Add more hair as needed to keep the cord of uniform diameter, and lay in new wisps when necessary to increase the length. Keep going in this way until a long cord is produced *four times the length of the rope desired*. Now hang this finished cord at its middle over the nail and twist the two strands together in the same way, making a two-strand rope. This completed, lay the rope over the spike again and repeat the process, producing a four-strand rope to finish the job. The loose end of the rope is terminated with a knot, usually a turkshead.

As compared to bast or bark ropes, horsehair ropes are rough and raggy, and much inclined to kink. For use as a lariat they are usually a little too light to make the long throws necessary in catch-roping.

The twisting of hair into rope by no means exhausts the possibilities in the use of horsehair in primitive crafts for beautiful and useful articles are created by plaiting, weaving, and half-hitching. Describing these skills, however, would take us afield from the more direct problems of woodcraft and campcraft.

PIONEER SHAVING HORSES

THE WOODCRAFT way is the simple way. Few tools, and simple tools, supplemented by a helpful gadget or two fashioned in the woods, plus a little ingenuity! The pioneer with few tools, sometimes none besides his ax, applied his intelligence to the task at hand and figured out some way to get it done. We need to know these simple ways of the pioneer, to possess ourselves of this priceless heritage of simple skills which the past has handed down to us, for we cannot take a carpenter's full chest of tools into the woods with us, nor a set of power machinery. And if we could, where would we find the joy of woodcraft or camping?

The shaving horse is such a product of man's ingenuity in the long ago—the predecessor of the present-day carpenter's elaborate work-bench. It is a log or heavy board contraption on which one sits while shaving down a stick with a drawknife.

It is a handy rig! Handier in fact than any modern hand device for the same purpose, and if one had both a fully equipped carpenter's bench and a shaving horse at his disposal, the chances are he would find many uses for the simple horse! It holds the stick for you as firmly as a vice while you shave it, and you can sit down while you work!

As surely as there was a spinning wheel in the corner, the old shaving horse was to be found by the woodpile behind the cabin. The spinning wheel is well nigh extinct, but the shaving horse is a healthy breed even to this day, to be seen behind the cabins throughout the wide frontier of the woods, whether in the North, the mountains of the West, the South or the East. And they are to be seen in the logging camps and all other establishments where work is to be done with rough wood, even if every modern hand tool is present, for the very good reason that the horse is handy, practical and efficient. That's why it has lived.

In a boy's camp we built one of these pioneer shaving horses merely as a building project—something for the boys to make—with no thought of it serving any good purpose other than to add a touch of true atmosphere to the woodcraft department. It would be an appropriate decoration! But once made, it found a score of uses, and at all hours of the day a boy could be seen comfortably seated on it shaving down his bow stave, his peace-pipestem, his boomerang stick, or a leg for his camp bench or stool. That was fifteen years ago and the old horse is still doing its regular daily turn throughout the summer. And when its legs refuse to stand up any longer, a new one will be built, for the shaving horse has become an indispensable institution in this camp.

The use of the shaving horse is the camp way of working. It belongs in camp. Let the city shop use its power machinery, the cabinetmaker his elaborate bench, but in camp let us insist on the shaving horse—it not only fits as though to the manner born but it does its work.

Let us make one:

How the Shaving Horse Is Made

We need three short sections of log, one ten inches in diameter and eight feet long, the second eight inches in diameter and twenty-seven inches long, and the third, six inches in diameter and twenty-five inches long. Any wood will do but soft stuff saves work and makes a horse lighter in weight and easier to move around—try *white cedar* or *chestnut.*

Split the ten-inch log in half using the methods described in Chapter VIII. From one of these halves we are to make the main bench of the horse—A in Figure 141. After the top surface has been smoothed up to remove the splinters and irregularities, cut the rectangular hole shown at x, making it two by six inches in size, by first drilling holes with a gouge and then cutting out the remainder of the wood and squaring up the corners with a chisel. Note that the hole is located thirty inches from one end of the log.

Now from the eight-inch log we must fashion the piece shown in B, Figure 141, which is twenty-seven inches in length. Note that this piece remains at full thickness for a distance of eight inches, then

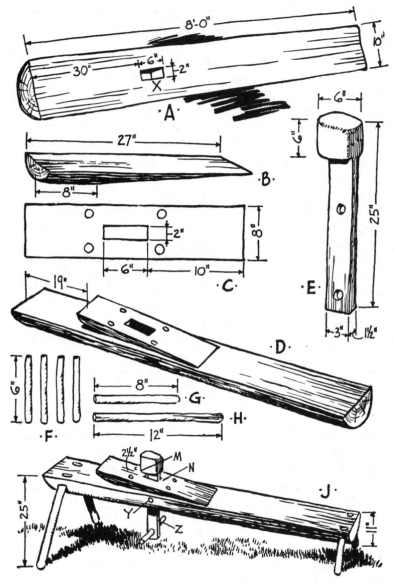

Figure 141. MAKING THE PIONEER SHAVING HORSE

tapers gradually down to a thin edge at the end. When so shaped up, we must cut the little rectangular hole shown in C, which drawing illustrates the top view of the piece we are making, cutting the hole two by six inches to exactly the same shape and size as the hole in the large log at A. Now lay this piece on the large log so that it sits as in D, Figure 141, placing the hole over the corresponding hole in the log below. Bore the four peg holes shown in C and D with a three-quarter-inch bitt and then drive the four six-inch pegs seen at F into the holes to hold the pieces together. Yes, of course, nails can be used in place of pegs, but they look out of place in a pioneer shaving horse --the pegging is a simple task after all and means doing the job right.

From the six-inch log we are now to make the clamp shown in E. Study the picture carefully—it shows the shape and size clearly. At a point six inches from the top the log is sawed to form the sharp shoulders illustrated, and the wood below is split out to a rectangular shape three inches wide and an inch-and-a-half thick. Round off the top shoulders as shown.

Insert this clamp, E, into the rectangular hole in the log so that it sits as shown in J. Now we must drive the pivot peg shown at Y in J, in such a way that the shoulder M is held exactly two-and-one-half inches above the log below it. To accomplish this, shove the vertical piece back firmly against the back side of the rectangular hole as at N, and then place a two-and-one-half-inch block beneath the shoulder so that the shoulder is exactly parallel with the surface of the bench beneath. With the vertical clamp held in this position, bore the hole at Y with a one-inch bitt extending it clear through the bench. Then remove the vertical clamp and enlarge the hole in it enough so that the one-inch peg when driven through will serve as a pivot permitting the clamp to rotate back and forth when moved. The peg is one inch in diameter and eight inches long, and is shown in G.

Now a hole must be bored two inches from the bottom of the vertical clamp in which a twelve-inch peg is driven to serve as a foot-rest—this is seen at Z in J.

Now install the legs to finish the shaving horse, drilling the holes with an inch-and-a-half auger and using two-inch hardwood for the legs. The high end of the horse should be elevated to twenty-five inches as seen in J, while the lower end is eleven inches from the ground. Sometimes we see shaving horses of this general type with

Figure 142. AN INDIAN USING HIS SHAVING HORSE BESIDE HIS WAGINOGAN

Figure 143. A WOODSMAN AND HIS SHAVING HORSE

the lower end resting on the ground and if that is preferred the main log from which the shaving horse is made should be ten feet long rather than eight.

In straddling the horse the rider sits on the high end facing the vise with his feet placed on the foot-rest, and so it is well to round off the edges of the log at the upper end so as to make them fit the shape of the legs more comfortably.

USING THE SHAVING HORSE

Mount the horse by straddling it at the upper end and facing the vise as the Indian is doing in Figure 142. Insert the stick on which you are to work under the shoulder at M in J, Figure 141. Place your two feet on the stirrups and press downward. This causes the shoulders at M to clamp down onto the stick and to grip it tight. The stick is now held fast so that you can go at it with the drawknife and shave it down to your heart's content. It was on such a contraption as this that the clapboards and shingles of the pioneer cabins were shaved down smooth after they were split out of the logs. And today we can find no handier rig for drawing down bow staves, calumet stems, or in fact sticks for any purpose that require shaving.

Not only the drawknife but the jackknife or sheath knife may be used to shave sticks on the horse. And the *crooked knife* of the Chippewas described in Chapter XIII is made to order for this kind of use, and is in fact a one-handled drawknife. When one is familiar with this exceedingly versatile and valuable knife and also with the shaving horse, he will find many tasks for the knife to perform in whittling, shaving, and carving sticks clamped tight by the vise of the horse.

ANOTHER SHAVING HORSE

The principle of the shaving horse is incorporated into many styles and shapes of supporting benches, for no two of these pioneer contraptions are the same, each woodsman constructing his according to his own fancy. The difference, however, is always in the supporting bench and never in the mechanism of the vise or clamp.

A shaving horse simpler and easier of construction than the one just described is illustrated in Figure 144, but in this arrangement we sit on the ground at the lower end of the bench, with legs straddling the log to reach the foot-rest, and thus proceed to do our shaving. The most of the shaving horses we encounter in the backwoods are of the type in which the operator sits on the ground, but for day-in-and-day-out use in all kinds of weather the elevated type is more promising of a dry seat.

Figure 144 illustrates rather clearly the construction of this horse. Two logs are needed, one ten inches in diameter and seven feet long, the other eight inches in diameter and two feet long. A thirty-inch section sawed off from the ten-inch log serves as the upright shown in A, and the remaining four-and-one-half feet is split to form the main bench, B in Figure 144. One end of this four-and-one-half-foot bench is cut down to a width of two inches as seen in D, which

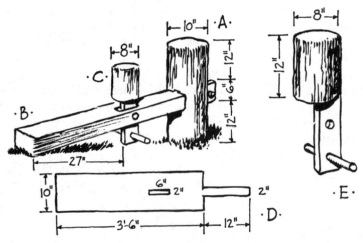

Figure 144. ONE SITS ON THE GROUND TO OPERATE THIS SHAVING HORSE

in turn is fitted into a hole cut through the upright twelve inches from the ground, as indicated in A. The other end of the bench rests on the ground.

The clamp is made exactly as in the previously described shaving horse and its shape and dimensions are illustrated in E—it remains at full width for a distance of twelve inches at the top and then is cut down to a thickness of an inch and a half and a width of three inches as illustrated. The pivot hole should be drilled so that the shoulder of the clamp will be elevated two-and-one-half inches above the surface of the shaving horse, and the lower extension should be of such length that it will barely clear the ground. It will be noted in Figure 144 that the foot-rest is twenty-seven inches from the lower end of the horse. If this places it so far away that your feet do not reach it conveniently as you sit on the ground at the end of the horse, bring it closer by sawing off a few inches from the lower end of the bench.

To operate this kind of a horse, sit on the ground with the lower end of the bench close up between your legs, bend your legs around the log and place your feet against the foot-rest. When the stick to be shaved is in position under the clamp, it will usually be found to be

Figure 145. ANOTHER STYLE OF SHAVING HORSE OPERATED BY SITTING
ON THE GROUND

at a convenient height for working, but should it prove to be too low for any particular job, a stick can be shoved under the lower end of the horse to elevate it a little.

In Figure 145 we have still another type of shaving horse which requires us to sit on the ground, but in this one we sit at the high end rather than the low. The high end is of such height that it comes to the level of your elbows as you sit on the ground, and the legs are spread wide enough so that you can shove your legs between them as you work. As a rule this type does not meet with as much favor as the one just described.

THE SPRING ROD

If there is much work to do on the shaving horse it pays to take time to erect the spring rod shown in Figure 146. Without the use of this rod the clamp or vise has to be lifted with the hand each time a stick is shoved under it, but with the spring rod attached the clamp springs erect as soon as the foot is taken off of the foot-rest and stays erect until foot pressure is applied again. Thus it is always ready to receive the stick.

Drill the hole in the bench about two feet behind the clamp and

insert a green, springy shoot in it as shown. Tie a strong string around
the top of the clamp and loop the other end of it over the top of the
rod, making the string of such length that the rod bends and exerts its
pressure on the clamp. When not in use the string should be slipped

Figure 146. Illustrating the Spring Rod That Holds the Clamp
Erect on a Shaving Horse

off so that the rod does not become permanently warped. In time, of
course, it will become so bent as to cease to exert pressure and will
have to be replaced with a new one.

SOME WOODCRAFT KNICKKNACKS

A LITTLE of this and that, mostly of a jackknife sort, all set forth in the woodcraft way—such is the nature of this chapter. Simple, elemental, primitive ways of making things—dishes, brooms, buttons, tools, war clubs, whistles, and so forth—gadgets and whatnots of this type and that for those who like the woods.

DECORATING WOOD BY SMOKING AND BURNING

The hand of the primitive is on it, the spirit of woodcraft within it, when naught but the smoke of the burning campfire is used to color it. No paints, no dyes to overadorn its elemental beauty, its primal simplicity! This is the ancient and truly primitive way. Its use is woodcraft.

There are two methods—fire coloration and burnt etching. Each has its separate uses, and each is appropriate for ornamenting the many articles described in this chapter.

Fire Coloration.—This is a simple smoking process that turns the wood brown. Let us do it the Chippewa way and that means the way of the northern woodland folk in general: Rub grease over the surface of the wood and then hold it over the flame of a slow fire of green hardwood. When the surface has turned uniformly dark withdraw it and *before it cools* rub it forcefully and briskly with a cloth. The result will be a brown ranging from medium to dark, approaching black, depending on how long it was held in the flame. Care must be taken not to burn or char the wood for the surface must remain smooth.

107

There are two ways to add highlights of beauty to objects so colored:

The first is to cut away small sections of the wood with a knife to allow the natural color of the wood to show. For example, if a wooden noggin or bowl is turned dark brown in the fire and a series of small scallops cut around its top edge, we have a light-colored scalloped border which stands out vividly and delightfully. Many old peace pipes achieved their rare beauty in this way. If a light-colored wood is used, so great is the contrast as to give the white sections a purity of such perfection that a mere finger touch seems to mean defilement!

The other method is to attach strips of bark or adhesive tape around the object before it is smoked and colored, and afterwards to remove them to reveal the contrasting whiteness of the areas beneath. The characteristic Chippewa design on the burl bowl in C, Figure 152, and also the plain line around the one at B, were done in this way. The Indian would cut out the design from buckskin and glue it on prior to smoking, but today we have the perfect material in adhesive tape—just cut it to the desired design and stick it on. Any of the designs recommended in Figure 125 for use on birch-bark makuks are appropriate for bowls or other wooden objects of the primitive type.

How did this interesting way of decorating originate? It has come down from those misty ancient times when sharp-edged tools were unknown and the Redman was forced to shape his wooden utensils by burning them. He would char the wood, rub it with buckskin, char it and rub it again, and so on until the object took on the desired form. That day is past, but the beauty of the old objects is still cherished and still achieved by the magic of the flame.

Burnt Etching.—Equally common and equally appropriate is this second of the Indian's methods of ornamenting by heat. It is to etch or burn the design on the wood with the hot point of an awl or wire. To prevent the hot point from slipping, the Indian would first scratch the design with the unheated point. Draw the design on in pencil, scratch over the lines with the awl or ice pick, and then etch it by retracing the lines with the point of the awl after it has been heated in the fire. The result is a brown line. This etched line can be turned to any color desired by scraping out the charred wood and then coloring the groove with ink or paint. Before the days of commercial paint the Indians used the juice of *bloodroot* to turn

etchings red. Several applications were necessary, each being allowed
to dry before the succeeding one was made.

NOGGINS

Noggins, the drinking mugs made from the burls, warts, or gnarls
that grow on trees, are an accepted institution in the American woods,
and for countless years have dipped the coolest of drinking water
from deep, shaded springs. A noggin attached to his belt was as
much a part of the typical equipment of the pioneer as was his
gun and powder-horn. In fact, so closely has the noggin become
related to pioneer life that we assume that it was an invention of
the early settlers, but the fact is that it was already an ancient institution when first the white man stepped ashore to view the new
world! In this as in many of his woodcraft skills, the pioneer was
a humble pupil sitting at the feet of those master woodsmen with
copper skins. The Indians of practically every tribe across the continent practiced the art of making cups from burls and so gave to us
the most colorful and picturesque of outdoor water mugs.

The knobs or bunions that grow on the trunks of trees are the
result of an early injury such as a hard bump, the loss of bark, or an
attack by insects. The gnarl is really scar tissue and is knotty in char-
acter. A burly old tree that is gnarled up in general may produce three
or four good burls, and again one may go a-foraging in the woods
for a couple of hours before finding anything resembling a good one.
But they are much more prevalent than we realize. Some kinds of
trees are given to growing burls—for example, *maple, birch, cherry,
apple* and *oak*. And happily, all of these woods produce excellent
noggins. The evergreens such as spruce and pine often grow warts
but they are invariably of inferior quality for noggin making. Un-
fortunately *hickory* does not produce many but when on occasion
we find one we have the making of a first-class noggin. And the same
can be said about *sycamore*.

The noggin is to be about the size of a drinking cup but the
burl selected should be slightly larger than that because it will diminish
as the bark is removed. Don't insist on a smooth, cup-shaped burl, for
irregularities do not detract from its practical value and add much
to its picturesque appearance.

Test the burl and see if it is healthy by scraping off the bark at
the end, for the rot to which these knobs are so susceptible will

usually make its presence known there. A rotted interior is a help, saving much hard whittling, but the shell must be sound. The burl should be removed with a saw and never chopped out. Saw very close to the tree trunk so as to leave a projection or lip on one side as seen in B, Figure 151—in order to accomplish this it is sometimes necessary to saw into the trunk slightly, as indicated by the dotted line in A.

If you would do the job in the easiest way, carve out the main body of the interior while the wood is still green, for dry hardwood makes a tough job of it. The roughest of the work done, it is well

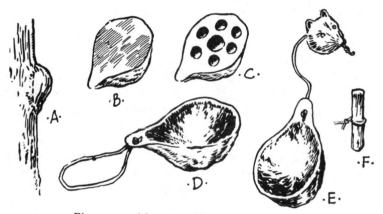

Figure 151. MAKING A NOGGIN FROM A BURL

to soak it in linseed oil or bacon fat and hang it up to dry out, to be smoothed up later. That is the Indian's way of doing it, the oil helping to prevent checking and cracking. Of course a dry burl can be manipulated if necessary.

Leave the bark on as a cover until the job is entirely completed, to protect the surface from becoming nicked, dented and dirty. Clamp the noggin in a vise, if one is to be had, and bore several holes in it with a bitt as shown in C, Figure 151. With a chisel cut out as much of the wood as possible, and then go at it with a gouge until the roughest of the wood has been cleaned out. The grain in a burl is irregular and the texture is knotty, so be sure your instruments are very sharp. The object is to turn the burl into a thin shell, the hollow interior conforming to the shape of the exterior. As the shell becomes thin we must work with exceeding caution in order not to punch a hole through it, and so the gouge should be abandoned in favor of a knife. If ever you will appreciate the crooked knife (see page 243) it is here, for the curved end of it is made to order for hollowing out such a curved hole as this. Just how thin the walls can be made will depend upon how close-grained or tightly knit the piece of wood happens to be, but any of the woods mentioned should produce a noggin with a wall not over an eighth of an inch thick at the top and a quarter of an inch thick at the bottom.

Ever present is the danger of the wood checking or cracking. This is the fate of many and many a noggin before it is finally completed. To prevent such a catastrophe, the noggin should be kept submerged in linseed oil when it is not being worked, which makes a messy job of it for the oil must be thoroughly wiped off before work can be started again, but it means to play safe. As a substitute for the oil, rub the wood thoroughly with bacon grease or meat drippings. The only other alternative is to keep the noggin in water.

When the interior has been excavated to the exact shape of the burl and the sides are as thin as they can be made with safety, apply sandpaper to the inside to smooth it up and then remove the bark from the outside with great caution. The bark off, soak the noggin in linseed oil overnight, when it is ready to dry for polishing with a piece of buckskin or leather. Do not use sandpaper on the outside but rather steel wool, or better still, leave it with its natural surface well polished with leather. The wood must be thoroughly dry to polish. Another method often used in finishing is to mix melted beeswax with turpentine, and rub the mixture well into both the outer and inner surfaces of the noggin.

A hole should now be drilled in the lip for the thong handle or toggle as seen in D and E, Figure 151. In respect to this no two noggins are alike and so the sky is the limit in using your imagination. A loop may be attached with a strip of buckskin or oiled rawhide, obtainable at the hardware store, as shown in D. When this loop is shoved under the belt the noggin is slipped through it. A more typically pioneer arrangement, however, is to attach the end of the thong to a toggle of some sort. This may be a plain stick an inch wide and an inch and a half long, as seen in F, which, when shoved up under the belt, will hold fast due to the pressure of the belt. Better, however, carve it in some way, as in E, Figure 151.

Most people like the noggin left in its natural finish but some prefer to shellac it or paint Indian symbols on it with lacquer. Better than painting is to color it in the Indian way by smoking and burning as described earlier in this chapter under the heading, "Decorating Wood by Smoking and Burning."

Burl Dippers.—To make the burl dipper of the Indian and pioneer we must saw the wart from the tree so as to leave a strip of wood attached to it for the handle—the dotted line in A, Figure 156, indicates the way. Then the burl is shaped up into the dipper pictured in C and hollowed out as in making the noggin.

Burl Bowls.—Not only cups but breakfast-food bowls and large serving dishes can be made from burls, indeed were so made by the

Figure 152. BURL BOWLS DECORATED BY THE FIRE-COLORATION METHOD

many Indian tribes across the land. Those of the Iroquois showed outstanding craftsmanship, while those of the northern Plains Indians and of the Utes and Piutes were more crude but none the less useful. The Pima and the Papago made these bowls from *mesquite*, the Hupa from *redwood*, and the southern Indians, although not confining their bowls to burlwood alone, relied on softwoods. And the tradition of these Indians in respect to wooden dishes was carried on by the white settlers who succeeded them in the various areas.

Warts aplenty of the size of breakfast-food bowls appear on trees and it is no uncommon sight to see one as large as a good-sized mixing bowl which would hold nigh on to a peck if hollowed out. We see burl bowls in B and C, Figure 152. That in A is a flat saucer excellent for an ash tray. Now the method of construction of these larger bowls is in no wise different from that of the noggins just described— the flat surface is broken up with holes made by a bitt and then the wood removed with chisel and gouge, to be smoothed up in the final stages with the Indian crooked knife or jackknife. Here, as with the noggin, the ever-present worry is checking and cracking, and so the bowl should be kept in water or better still in linseed oil except when it is being worked, and the final product should receive a good soaking for at least a day in linseed oil, or several rubbings with grease from bacon or other meat. These food bowls can be flattened on the bottom if necessary so that they will sit level on the table. The finishing polish is given just as in the case of the noggin.

The decorations on the bowls in Figure 152 are applied by the fire-coloration method described earlier in this chapter.

Wooden Dishes

Differing from the bizarre and picturesque mugs and bowls of the noggin type, these dishes are more or less regular and uniform in shape and are whittled out of a solid block of wood. The dishes of the Chippewas were made from *ash*, *maple* and *birch*, and those of the Choctaws and Cherokees from *tupelo*, the latter being far-famed for the craftsmanship they show.

While any close-grained piece of hardwood may be whittled into a cup, saucer, plate, or bowl, the experience of the northern Woodland Indians proves that the best wood is obtained from the trunk just above the level of the ground where it begins to spread out into the roots. The Chippewas preferred maple and birch thus obtained. Plates and saucers are easy, and a cup on the order of a good-sized coffee cup becomes a simple task, curved handle and all, provided you have a crooked knife (page 61) with which quickly to scoop it out. However, it can be done with a jackknife by starting the bore with a bitt.

In Figure 153 we have samples of dishes made in this way, together with a tray of a more crude variety of the type used by the northern Woodland Indians for cutting and mixing tobacco. These are all made of birch or maple, the cups and bowls being hollowed out roughly while the wood is green, then soaked for a few hours in linseed oil and hung up to dry for a few days, when they can be whittled down to careful shape and smoothed up. To complete the thinly whittled sides while the wood is green will doubtless lead to checking.

Bamboo Cups.—As neat and trim a cup as one could ever want to use is handed down to us in the cane or bamboo cups of the southern Indians. The node or joint of the bamboo makes a watertight bottom, so all one has to do is to saw off the bamboo to the proper length and round off the edges to produce the cup shown in A, Figure 154. A large joint of bamboo will of course be necessary to make a cup of sufficient width. Tumblers, too, of pleasing proportion, light in weight, and delightful in every respect, are made from bamboo. We

Figure 153. WOODEN DISHES

see one of these in B, Figure 154. And if an inch-wide strip of bamboo is left extending upward above the cup for a few inches, we have the dipper shown in C.

By boring a little hole through the upper edge of the bamboo or cane cup and attaching a thong to it, we can carry the cup on the belt after the fashion of the noggin of the pioneers.

Cocoanut Shell Bowls.—Serviceable dishes of various shapes and sizes may be made from cocoanut shells—eating bowls, saucers, small trays, cups or sugar bowls, depending upon the shape into which the cocoanut is sawed.

Shell Bowls.—Without any work at all and used just as they are picked up, ordinary seashells make excellent camp saucers, cups or bowls depending upon their size and shape. These were much used by the Indians and were frequently shaped up to a more convenient form by chipping.

Milk skimmers were synonymous with shells in the pioneer household. A clamshell or sea shell of similar general shape is made to order for the purpose.

Gourd Dishes.—See Chapter XXII.

Horn Cups.—See Chapter XX.

Bamboo Salt-and-Pepper Shakers

Salt and pepper are a nuisance on a camping trip. The salt picks up moisture no end and not even a watertight food-bag will keep it dry. While the main supply should be carried in a metal can with a screw top, the bamboo salt-and-pepper shaker shown at D, Figure 154, is the perfect rig for use at mealtime. It is light in weight, watertight, and fits conveniently into the cooking-utensil bag.

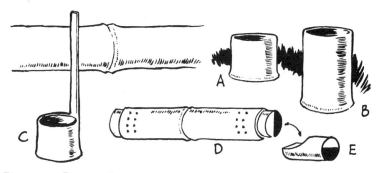

Figure 154. Bamboo Cup, Tumbler, Dipper and Salt-and-Pepper Shaker

A piece of bamboo or cane containing a node or joint is needed, measuring an inch to an inch and a half in diameter. Saw it off two-and-a-half inches from the joint on one side, and three-and-a-half inches on the other side, making it six inches over all, the short end to be used for pepper and the long end for salt. Now bore in their respective ends the tiny holes of the proper size for salt and pepper as indicated. The corks, made from basswood, cedar, or other soft woods, are whittled to fit very snugly, and then are cut away on one side as shown in E. *When the cork is inserted it may be turned to close the holes, or turned in the opposite direction to open the holes for use.* It is well to paint one side of the cork as shown in E, so that you can tell at a glance whether or not the holes are sealed. If you choose, the pepper end may be painted one color and the salt end another color so that there will be no confusion as to which end is which, but this is really unnecessary because the pepper end, being shorter, is easily identified.

Spoons and Ladles

When first the white man presented himself to the Indians there was much behind-his-back mirth among the red folks over the diminutive size of the spoons he used, and the many trips the spoon had to make between the bowl and the mouth. The spoons of the Indians were large, a sort of a combined spoon and ladle, the smaller ones holding about the quantity of a present-day tablespoon.

In A and B, Figure 155, we have the typical wooden spoons of the Timber Indians and of the roving white settlers who adopted the red way. These hold about the amount of present-day tablespoons while those at C, D and E were drawn from ladles used in serving and cooking, ranging in width at the bowl from three to ten inches, that in D being more of a dipper. All these were Indian made.

Let us make the spoon shown in B, which is typical in shape and appropriate in size for eating. By using *basswood* or *cedar* this becomes an easy enough task, but the Chippewas relied on *birch* or *maple*, preferably the latter, to make a spoon exceedingly strong and capable of standing much battering. Let us first describe the Chippewa way:

It was from the butt of the sugar maple that the Indian liked to obtain the wood, cutting it just where the trunk spreads out into the roots at the ground level. Here the grain turns outward into a curve corresponding to the curve of the bark and so the wood is made to order for fashioning the spoon. Such bird's-eye spoons seldom break.

Square up the block to a size measuring 7½ by 2 by 2½ inches, as seen in F and G, Figure 155, and draw the shape of the spoon on its sides. We save much work and grief as we saw out the block roughly along the dotted lines, for maple is hard to whittle. However, do not saw off the triangular piece below the bowl, but rather leave the block as in H until the bowl of the spoon is scooped out—it is less liable to split under the pressure of whittling that way. Note in B that the handle of the spoon is wide and is slightly scooped out throughout its length.

Remember that green wood whittles much easier than dry, but cannot be scraped and polished so well. So complete all that you can with the knife, then rub linseed oil or grease from fat drippings into it and let it dry a few days. Finish by scraping it with a piece

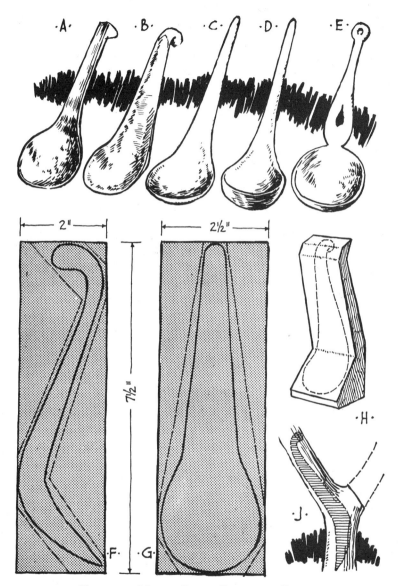

Figure 155. MAKING INDIAN SPOONS AND LADLES

of broken glass and sanding it, then rub in more linseed oil and polish with a rough cloth.

Another convenient way of making a spoon from a natural curve is to use a crotched stick as illustrated in J, Figure 155. One prong of the crotch is cut away and then the spoon is whittled out as indicated in the drawing.

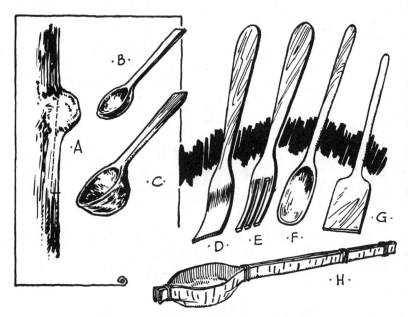

Figure 156. MADE FROM WOOD AND BARK

From these instructions the dimensions of the large ladles can easily be worked out. If maple proves too difficult, try *basswood, cedar* or *tulip.*

Small burls and knots were also used by the Indians in making spoons, that shown in B, Figure 156, being typical. The process is identical with that described for making a burl dipper, the gnarl being sawed off so as to leave a handle attached, as indicated by the dotted line in A, Figure 156, and then the spoon shaped up and hollowed out as in making a noggin.

In the southern mountain regions, *mountain laurel* was so extensively used as a source of spoons by the Indians that it has often been called *spoonwood* in that area. This wood may be whittled out into a present-day spoon of the salad-bowl type as in F, Figure 156. D indicates a sort of curved ladle that does excellent service in a salad bowl.

A flapjack turner can be made from any hardwood by merely shaping it as in G, leaving it entirely flat throughout.

Birch-Bark Spoons.—While on their long treks the northern Timber Indians frequently extemporized a spoon by folding a sheet of thin birch-bark as shown in H, Figure 156. Needless to say this was a temporary arrangement to be discarded when next the party went on its way. A slender strip of basswood bark or a piece of string

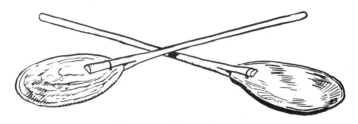

Figure 157. SHELL SPOONS

will hold the spoon in shape. See Chapter X for the details of the craft of working with birch-bark.

Shell Spoons.—All there is to it is to split a twig and attach it over the end of the half of a clamshell as in Figure 157. Mark the edges of the twig on the shell, bore two little holes either side using any pointed instrument such as an awl or the leather tool on a scout knife, and then tie the twig in place with sinew or string.

Other Kinds of Spoons.—See Chapter XX for horn spoons and Chapter XXII for gourd spoons.

Wooden Forks.—Wooden forks for eating are not extensively used in camp, but delightfully appropriate salad-bowl forks for use at home may be made from *mountain laurel, beech* or *ash.* That shown in E, Figure 156, is the simplest, being identical in shape with the salad scoop or spoon in D except for the cut-outs forming the prongs. The use of *toasting forks* over the campfire is described in Chapter VII.

WOODEN NAPKIN-RINGS

Mountain laurel is the traditional wood for the making of napkin-rings but any of the closely knit hardwoods may be employed, such as *birch, beech, ash,* or *cherry.* Roots are usually considered superior, but either a branch or a root measuring an inch and three-quarters to two inches in diameter may be used. Cut off a piece two inches long and wrap it tightly throughout its entire length with cord or adhesive tape. Place it in a vise, tightening the clamp just enough to hold the

Figure 158. WOODEN NAPKIN-RINGS, B AND C DECORATED BY FIRE COLORATION

wood secure and not exert any undue pressure. Now using a sharp bitt about three-quarters of an inch in diameter and working very slowly and cautiously, drill a hole through the center. This done, remove the remainder of the wood with a sharp jackknife until it has been reduced to a thin shell with walls an eighth of an inch thick. Now remove the string or tape, thin down the edges and smooth up in general. Not all woods can be thinned down as much as mountain laurel without breaking, and it is often wise to leave the bark on as an additional protection.

For the ornamentation of woodcraft napkin-rings three methods may be used—carving, burnt etching and fire coloration. Try smoke coloration for an effect that is different yet thoroughly appropriate and in harmony with the Indian way—the decorations shown in B and C, Figure 158, were applied in this way. The method is described earlier in this chapter under the heading, "Decorating Wood by Smoking and Burning," which discussion also described the appropriate burnt-etching process.

In A, Figure 158, we have a napkin-ring in its natural color with a scalloped effect carved on the ends. When it comes to carving the napkin-rings the opportunities are limitless—use your imagination.

Burl Napkin-Rings.—The bizarre and irregular quality that makes noggins so interesting recommends the use of burls for napkin-rings. Saw off the tip of a small burl *before the burl itself is removed from the tree*, then cut off the remainder and clamp in a vise. Drill a hole through the center with a brace and bitt, and then proceed to hollow out the center following the general directions given for the making of noggins earlier in this chapter, including the soaking in linseed oil to prevent cracking and splitting.

Other Types of Napkin-Rings.—See Chapter XX, "Horn," and Chapter XXII, "Gourds."

BREAD AND MEAT BOARDS

Make a bread board for the camp dining table, a meat-cutting board for the camp kitchen, or a dough-mixing board, by sawing a log obliquely as shown in Figure 159. Any log may be used but

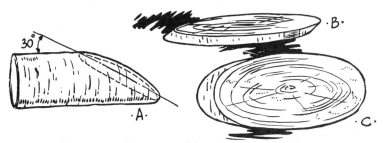

Figure 159. BREAD AND MEAT BOARDS FROM BIRCH

white birch is to be preferred—this wood is excellent for cutting and its bark most attractive. The board is one inch thick and sawed off at an angle of thirty degrees, as indicated in the illustration. When so cut we have an oval board that is twice as long as it is wide. For a *bread board* a log seven inches in diameter is just the right size, making an oval board seven by fourteen inches; for a *meat-cutting board* a nine-inch log should be used, and for a *dough-mixing board*, a twelve-inch log to produce a board twelve by twenty-four inches in size.

Boards cut in this way not only find many uses around the camp kitchen but are frequently employed for *signs* and other ornamentation around camps and summer places.

Paper Knives

Whittling is synonymous with the open spaces. Whether pioneer, cowboy, prospector, lumberjack, or sourdough of the Far North, we find him idling with his pocketknife and a piece of wood, perhaps carving out something or perhaps just whittling. And all of us seem to get that way once we emerge into the unhampered life of the woods, free to live as we please.

The perennial popularity of sheath knives makes understandable the ever-present tendency of boys to whittle out knives and daggers of wood, a tendency which can be given practical import by fashioning paper knives or letter openers. This is an excellent introduction to knife-craft.

Paper knives seem to divide themselves into two classes—*first*, those which are made of straight-grained softwood and rely on the natural finish of the wood in both the blade and handle, the blade being carved somewhat to the shape of a conventional knife, such as those in the top row in Figure 160; and *second*, those which are whittled out of a rough branch of a tree retaining all of the knobs, irregularities, and rough features of the bark—those of the bottom row in Figure 160 are of this type.

Those in the top row are much the easier to make but less efficient as paper knives. Make them from *white cedar, white pine, basswood*, or other softwoods. Thin down the piece to three-sixteenths of an inch in thickness and draw the outline of the knife with pencil. The handle is no thicker than the blade in these simplest of knives, and so all there is to it is to cut out the shape of the knife and thin the edge of the blade down to a cutting edge. Sand it well, rub it with fine emery cloth, and put on the polish with a rough cloth or piece of leather. The decorations on the handles of A, B, and E, Figure 160, are painted, while those on C, D, F, and G are carved in low relief and the features then brought out and strengthened with paint. Burnt etching as described earlier in this chapter is also very effective on these knives. In H and J we have paper knives made to resemble *canoe paddles* and painted with typical canoe-paddle decorations. *Always avoid names, initials and other modern symbols.*

On softwood knives of this sort lacquer should not be used but rather watercolor, and this sparingly—just enough to bring out the design. Fix permanently by painting or spraying with a fixative after

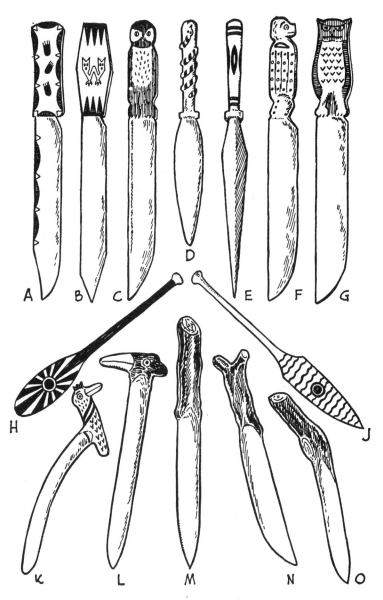

Figure 160. PAPER KNIVES

the coloring has dried. The knives are usually left in the natural finish of the wood without shellac, oil, or any other type of polish.

Better than these softwood knives are those with rough-bark handles as seen in the bottom row in Figure 160—they keep an edge better, are more attractive, and look appropriate on any desk no matter how elaborate it is. The rough-bark handle stands out in delightful contrast to the finished and polished blade. For these we need hard or medium-hard wood and, while any such wood can be used, the attractiveness of the knife will be greatly enhanced if we select one with a pleasing grain—*walnut, white oak, maple* and *red cedar* are excellent. *Birch* and *rhododendron* make strong knives with light-colored blades which keep an edge well, but are less attractive in grain.

Cut the stick to the length of the knife desired and mark the line between blade and handle. With a sharp knife thin the blade down to a thickness of an eighth of an inch and keep it at this thickness until the taper to the point begins. Scrape it with a piece of broken glass, smooth it up with a fine emery cloth, and then rub it well with a rough cloth or a piece of buckskin or leather. Leave the bark on the handle, merely smoothing it up. By keeping your eye open for knobs and irregularities, and using your imagination, all sorts of interesting, bizarre effects can be created in the handle.

These knives should not be painted but merely polished. Don't rush this polishing task, for no amount of shellac or oil will cover up a half-done job. The final finish may be applied by rubbing with linseed oil or white shellac. To do this, place a rag over the finger, dip it in the shellac or oil and rub with much pressure; when it dries apply another coat and thus continue until a high polish is achieved. Another interesting way to finish these knives is to use the Indian method of fire coloration as described earlier in this chapter. When so burnt or smoked to turn the blade dark, a little whittling here and there will cause the light, natural color of the wood to stand out in striking contrast. It may then be polished in the usual way.

WOODCRAFT BROOMS

Besides the home-made *shaved brooms* which played such an important role in the pioneer cabin of years past and which still hold sway in the inaccessible regions, there are four other types of brooms used in woodcraft—the *switch broom*, the *grass broom*, the *pine-needle* broom, and the *corn-husk* broom. Let us look at these in order, starting with the famed shaved broom.

The Shaved Broom.—Here we have as interesting a craft as can be found in the woods and one that will produce first-class and long-lived brooms, either tiny ones of the whisk-broom type, medium-sized ones for use around the fireplace, or large ones for the floor. The years have identified these brooms with the early settlers, but here again, as in most of the pioneer's skills, the craft was borrowed outright from the Indian woodsmen to whom these sweepers were household articles for—we know not how long.

You will need a good jackknife with a thin blade and a sharp one. The traditional wood is *yellow birch*—in fact this tree has been so intimately identified with brooms that it is often called broom-wood. Other woods which make first-class brooms are *blue beech, hickory, witch-hazel, white oak, ash,* and *elm.*

Let us make the little whisk broom shown in C, Figure 161, and then take up the construction of the larger broom in E which is of the size of an ordinary house broom.

Find a green stick measuring twelve inches in length and about an inch and a half in diameter. Remove the bark as shown in A—peel it from the five-inch section marked *z* and also from the five-and-one-half-inch section marked *x*, but leave it attached to the half-inch strip at *y* and the inch strip at *w*. Cut a shallow V-shaped groove throughout the length of *z* in order to give us a chance to shave off the thin splints at a slight angle into the wood. Now, using the point of the knife, strip the shavings or splints from the edge of this groove, continuing all the way around the stick, but being cautious to leave them attached firmly at *y*, at which point the bark strip creates a shoulder that serves to terminate the splints. Continue to remove the splints layer after layer until the mass of shavings makes it difficult to do more, then cut out the remaining core of wood. Skillful workers can often reduce the entire core to splints. The next task is similarly to shave down the section marked *x*, but shaving this time in the *opposite direction* and again leaving the splints attached at *y*—study the drawing at B and you will get the idea. When this section has been reduced to a core a half inch in diameter *the shavings are bent downward over the top of the z shavings and bound there* with a wet rawhide thong or soft wire, as shown in C. Finish the broom by smoothing up the handle as in C, drilling a hole at the end, and in-

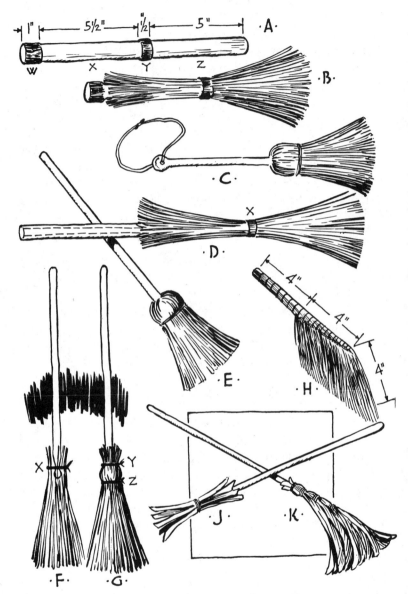

Figure 161. WOODCRAFT BROOMS

serting a loop of string by which to hang the broom. The end of the bristles should be trimmed to approximately the same length.

The full-sized broom for the floor shown in E is made from a green pole of yellow birch or one of the other woods named above, *six feet long* and *five inches in diameter*. Peel the pole except for the two-inch strip marked *x*, which is fifteen inches from the butt end. The broom is made exactly as in the case of the whisk broom just described; first shave up the butt end leaving the splints attached at *x* and cutting out the core when the shaving can be carried no farther: then, beginning *eighteen inches* above the bark strip marked *x* shave the second set of splints in the *opposite direction*, leaving them attached at *x*. When the core has been reduced to the size of an ordinary broomstick, double this second or upper set of bristles down over the lower bunch, as seen in E, and bind the two sets of splints tightly together with a wet rawhide thong, soft wire, or very strong string. Whittle down the large end of the stick to broomstick size and smooth up the handle with sandpaper to finish the job.

Switch Brooms.—These switch or twig brooms so widely used among the Indians are much more quickly constructed but for efficiency and durability are not to be regarded in the class with the shaved brooms. Secure a stick of the size of an ordinary broomstick and whittle one end of it down to a knob as seen at *x* in F, Figure 161, to provide a shoulder to hold the twigs in place. Using slender *willow* or *birch* switches, lay a layer over the whittled end of the stick and tie as seen in F, then place another layer on top and tie, and thus continue, *tying each layer separately* until the broom is of the desired size. Then tie the bundle again at *z* in G, and trim off the ends of the twigs to uniform length to complete the job.

Grass Brooms.—The Indian grass broom was more or less a temporary arrangement but nevertheless a good one. This is a hand broom for the floor and the fireplace, used without a handle. Secure a bundle of broom-sedge or other long grass or grain, and bind the butts together with a wrapping of cord, as in A, Figure 162. The Pueblo and Plains Indians would bind the grass about four inches from the butt end, and then use the butt end to comb their hair and the long end to sweep the floor! See "Hairbrushes and Combs" in this chapter.

Pine-Needle Brooms.—As beautiful a little broom as one could hope to use can be made from pine needles if one is in the southern area where the long-leaf pine (*Pinus palustris*) or the slash pine (*Pinus caribaea*) is available, the needles of these trees often measuring upwards of twelve inches in length. After the bunches have been gathered and spread out in the sun and wind to dry for a few days, the needles will pull loose very readily.

These twelve-inch needles may be gathered into a compact bundle measuring an inch in thickness and wrapped with string for a distance of four inches at the butt end to form a whisk broom without a handle, or they may be bound to a stick as in making the switch broom shown in F and G, Figure 161. The best type of pine-needle whisk broom, however, is that shown in H, Figure 161. Pick out a bundle of thirty-six needles twelve inches long and tie with the end of a long string four inches from their tip end. Then place another bundle of thirty-six needles below the first and wrap the string around both bundles about a quarter of an inch from the first wrapping. Then add a third bundle of the same size below the second, and continue thus until about sixteen bundles have been laid in, or until the wrapped part of the broom becomes four inches long—study H and the method of construction will become clear. Then continue to wrap the string around the butt end of the bundle to form a handle four inches long and about one inch in diameter. Shellac the handle to set the string.

Corn-Husk Brooms.—Corn husks are exceedingly strong and fibrous, so much so that it is impossible to tear them crosswise, and so have the stamina to do good service when fashioned into a broom. They are ideal for a fireplace broom. Gather the husks in the fall and winter, or any time after the green leaves have turned to brown, using field corn if possible because the husks are more substantial than those from sweet corn. The coarse-grained leaves of the outer layer are the best for brooms. Sort out three dozen of the longest ones obtainable and trim off the thick ends with scissors. For the broomstick use a thirty-inch stick of the size of an ordinary broomstick and whittle one end of it down to a knob to form a shoulder as seen at *x* in F, Figure 161.

Our corn-husk broom is seen at J and K. Place a dozen corn husks over the end of the stick and bind them at the middle with soft wire, as seen in J. Now place a second bundle of twelve husks beneath the first and bind to the stick about an inch from the first. Install a third bundle in the same way and then wrap the ends of all three bunches with an additional wrapping as illustrated in K. If available, wet rawhide thongs may be used for wrapping to better advantage than the wire. Trim off the ends of the corn husks evenly and the broom is ready to use.

Corn husks take dye beautifully and can be colored to any shade as in dying cloth. By painting the broomstick in various colors and dying the corn husks in a blending shade, a most attractive pioneer broom results.

HAIRBRUSHES AND COMBS

For a hairbrush use a dry *corncob*—it serves the purpose better than one might think! Part the hair with a pointed stick in Indian fashion, then brush it up with the cob.

Better is the *grass hairbrush* of the Pueblo and Plains Indians already referred to under "Grass Brooms," it being used by the Indians as a combined hairbrush and broom. It is pictured in A, Figure 162, a compact bundle of broom-sedge or other long, stiff grass or grain, three inches in diameter, bound together about four inches from the butt end. It is this three-inch butt-end that makes an efficient hairbrush. The Indians would use the other or long end to sweep the floor, but for our purpose the long end can be cut away as in B, retaining the wrapped butts only for use on the hair.

Figure 162. GRASS BROOM AND GRASS HAIRBRUSH

For a comb a *porcupine tail* bound to a stick was much used on the Plains in the early days.

WOODCRAFT MOPS

The mop of the backwoods is made from corn husks. We see it in Figure 163. The board is three-fourths of an inch thick and about seven inches wide, cut out to a circular shape if you have the facilities, or the corners sawed off to an octagonal shape, or just left square as in the illustration. Bore the handle hole at a slight angle, fit the handle to it, and glue with waterproof glue. Then bore the holes for the corn husks as shown using a three-eighths inch bitt.

There are two methods of attaching the corn husks: The first is to force them up through the hole for half their length and then to force the tops down through the next hole, as illustrated in Figure 163, using a wire hook to assist in the process. The second way is merely to force the husks through the hole until the tips protrude about an inch above the board. What prevents them pulling out? Corn husks swell and expand when wet, and a few minutes in the mop pail will fix them securely. Scrubbing mops like these are never used dry anyway.

Figure 163. MOP MADE FROM CORN HUSKS

CAMP WASHBOARDS

A washboard for scrubbing clothes can be extemporized from a slab as shown in Figure 164. Select a wide slab of hardwood that has a smooth surface after the bark has been peeled. Cut a series of grooves across it to form the ribbed surface, rounding off the sharp corners carefully. A wood rasp is a handy tool for this but it can be done with a jackknife and chisel if one has plenty of time.

Clothespins.—Just split the end of a half-inch green stick, removing the bark at the split end so as not to soil or color the clothes. Such clothespins must be pulled open with the fingers each time they are used.

SOAP AND SOAP SUBSTITUTES

To find oneself in the woods without soap shows poor planning, but there are substitutes to be had for the finding, and ways of making soap itself if necessary.

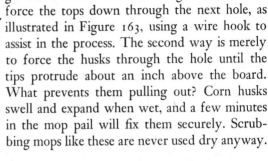

Figure 164. WASHBOARD MADE FROM A SLAB

Lathering Plants.—Some plants will provide lather and so serve as a first-class substitute for soap, provided they can be located when needed. Probably the best of these is *bouncing bet* or *soapwort* (*Saponaria officinalis*), a native of Europe and

Asia long popular in the flower gardens of this country, from which it has escaped to become a common wild plant. This contains a large amount of *saponin* and thus lathers up readily, not only cleaning clothing but adding a luster as well. It was much used as soap during the Middle Ages and was preferred to soap by the pioneer house-wives for washing fine silks.

The roots and even the leaves of the *buckeyes* will provide some-what of a lather when the hands are rubbed across them, and likewise will the seed clusters of the *New-Jersey-tea.*

The bulb of the California soaproot (*Chlorogalum pomeridianum*) produces an abundant lather and was the soap of the California Indians and early settlers, the Indians calling the plant *amole*. In the Southwest the roots of *yucca* and *bear-grass*, and also the fruit of the *wild pumpkin*, are said to possess similar qualities.

Ash Water.—This is the Woodland Indian's method of preparing water for washing when soap was to be had. Hardwood ashes from the fireplace were placed in water and boiled, the pot allowed to stand and the weak lye water drained off. Clothes were washed in such water, the test against too strong a lye solution being whether or not the hand could be inserted in it. Dishes likewise were washed in it after first being scoured with sand.

Woodcraft Scouring Agents.—For the scouring of greasy skillets, plates and pots, the *sand* of the lake shore leaves little to be desired—it cleans out the grease, grinds loose attached particles, and leaves the pans dry and clean for their final soap bath or rinsing. A *corncob* used with the sand is an ideal combination. *Dry ashes* from the campfire are also an excellent cleansing agent, inferior to sand for scouring but possessing greater cleansing properties. If no soap is to be had, first scour with sand if possible, then rub the ashes on the dampened pans with a cloth.

The stalks of the *scouring-rush* or *horsetail* (*Equisetum*) with their sandpaper-like covering are also excellent and have long been used by woodsmen, both red and white. They are particularly effective for removing masses of badly caked material in the pans and the thicker layers of black that form on the bottoms of the pots. Their rigidity is due to the abundance of the mineral silica contained within them.

Making Soap.—Two things are needed—a good quantity of *hardwood* ashes from the campfire and some melted animal fat (not pork).

Put the ashes in the kettle with just enough water to cover nicely, and boil. Allow the ashes to settle and then pour off the water. It will take a good quantity of this lye or potash water and if sufficient ashes are not available, the process can be repeated from day to day as a new supply accumulates in the campfire. Now boil this lye water until the greater part of the water has evaporated and a very strong lye solution is left—the early settler's test as to the proper strength of the solution was whether or not it would float an egg. Now mix the animal fat and the hot lye water and stir it well as it boils until it is about as thick as mush. When this concoction cools we have soft soap.

To turn it into hard soap, a quantity of salt should be added just as it is taken off of the fire. About two heaping tablespoons of salt to a quart of the soap mixture will be the right proportion, or a teacup full to a gallon. It is well to pour this mixture into a shallow tray for cooling so that it can be cut or broken into cakes later on. If we will follow the pioneer custom of leaving the soap outdoors until needed, the cakes will become increasingly hard as time goes by.

As a substitute for the boiling process to produce the lye the settlers would sometimes place the ashes in a tilted box and periodically pour a small amount of water over them, allowing the strong lye seepage to drip into a kettle placed beneath. However, the boiling method is quicker.

Buttons of Wood

The age-old button of the Woodland Indians, the simplest of all buttons, is seen in A, Figure 165. It is merely a short piece of twig with a groove cut around its middle in which the string or thread is tied and then sewed to the clothing. This is a good, practical button and by no means an unornamental one when used on camp clothing—it adds plenty of the right kind of atmosphere. In length the twig buttons can be considerably longer than the length of the buttonhole and still be buttoned if inserted endwise.

The little buttons shown in B, Figure 165, are made by sawing off crosswise sections from a branch of any close-knitted wood with a solid heart. In the southern mountain regions, *mountain laurel and rhododendron* are extensively used for this purpose; other suitable woods are ash, beech, birch, wild black cherry, apple, black walnut. These buttons are excellent for outdoor shirts. They may range in size from a half inch in diameter upward, but the best width for use on a coat is about three-quarters of an inch. Regardless of the diameter, they should be a quarter of an inch in thickness. The branch from which they are made does not necessarily need to be perfectly round, for irregularity always adds much in the way of

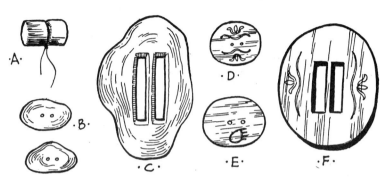

Figure 165. WOODEN BUTTONS

atmosphere. The holes are bored with a fine drill and the surface polished with fine emery cloth and finished by rubbing with buckskin.

Appearing at C in Figure 165 is a belt buckle made from a cross-section of rhododendron which relies on friction to hold the belt in place. This measures 2½ by 3¼ inches, and its thickness is ⅜ inch. A delightful combination results when one of these buckles is used in connection with the buttons shown in B.

Now in D and E, Figure 165, we have buttons whittled out from a thin board. These measure three-sixteenths of an inch in thickness and are usually slightly oblong in shape, those for coats measuring about an inch by an inch and a quarter, the grain of the wood going the long way of the button. *Walnut, maple* and *cherry* are the best woods because of their delightful grain and color when polished. The belt buckle in F, made in the same way, measures 2 by 2¼ inches. The making of such buckles and buttons as these is a typical craft among the southern mountain people who usually ornament them with incised drawings done with the point of a penknife, samples of which appear. The burnt-etching process described earlier in this chapter is also an appropriate means for decorating these buttons.

Camp Ladders

They are not really ladders at all in the sense that we think of today but they get us up to the tree house, the roof of a building,

Figure 166. Ladders

or the side of a rock precipice on a portage just a well as any modern ladder. There are two types, the simplest being a single pole with notches cut on either side of it as shown in A, Figure 166, which we grasp with our arms as in climbing a tree and proceed to elevate ourselves. More commonly seen and more convenient, however, is a pair of poles set up about twelve inches apart as in B. When these two poles are set nearly erect we have a ladder but when they are leaned at an angle of about forty-five degrees to the wall, we have the stairway of the early pioneer cabin.

Such ladders as these were used in the dome-shaped earth lodges of the Sioux and Mandan Indians years ago, and in the somewhat similar lodges of some of the tribes of the Northwest Coast, connecting the floor with the hole that served as an entrance in the middle of the roof.

Camp Pincers

Pincers or pliers of the type we use today the Indians knew not, nor can serviceable ones be made successfully in the woods. However, the Indian did make a kind of "pincer" out of a straight stick, the simple principle of which should be known by every camper should the emergency arise that would demand it. Secure a stick of very strong and tough wood such as *hickory, elm,* or *oak,* thirteen inches long and an inch in diameter after the bark had been removed. Whittle this to an oblong shape, about three-quarters of an inch in diameter the short way and an inch in diameter the long way. Three inches from one end cut a notch or groove all the way around it in which a wet rawhide thong is wrapped very tightly around the stick and tied. Now split the other end of the stick for half its length—this split should end an inch or two from the rawhide wrapping, the wrapping being designed to prevent the split from extending itself too far with use. Now flatten off one side of the stick at the split end only, as indicated in Figure 167, so that the upper split section is about twice the thickness of the lower at the extreme end.

Figure 167. CAMP "PINCERS"

To use the "pincers": Spread open the split with the fingers, insert in the crack the object to be held, and then grasp the stick with both hands and squeeze. There is no lever principle as in ordinary pliers and therefore the only pressure that can be obtained is that applied by the fists. A rig of this type is much used among the Indians for stretching hide: after the jaws are closed on the hide, the hide is wrapped around the stick so as to obtain a greater purchase, whereupon it is pulled and stretched with much greater pressure than could be applied by means of the hands alone. The "pincers" shown in Figure 167 are part of the equipment of an old Chippewa water-drum, used to tighten the buckskin head of the drum when it is being tuned up for use.

Small, wooden tweezers may be made in the same way from small twigs of hardwood.

SHELL TWEEZERS

How does it happen that we never see an Indian with a beard? Doesn't he have whiskers? Yes, of a straggly sort, but we never see pictures of an ancient Redman with even a scrawny beard—how did he shave? He didn't—*he pulled his whiskers out with tweezers,* and he does so to this day in many of those tribes that have succeeded in retaining their own culture. And the instrument used to accomplish this is usually a *clamshell* with the two halves still hinged together. These tweezers are excellent for all fine work since they have thin, smooth edges that clamp tightly on the tiniest object. Just close the lips of the shell on the object and pinch with the fingers.

WOODCRAFT AWLS

The awl of the far woods is the splint from a deer's leg. This is ready to use the minute it is taken off and requires no fixing up other than perhaps to wrap the butt end with cloth for a hand hold. It was with these sharp awls that the Timber Indians punched holes in buckskin for the lacings and in sheets of birch-bark for the binding thongs, and with them also they drilled holes in wood. These are usable wherever pointed instruments are needed.

PUMP DRILLS

The clever pump drill which so handily drills small holes for us in the woods is the result of a long evolution of drills among the Indians. The first drill was an awl—a splint from a deer's leg which was held in the hand and revolved by wrist motion to drill a hole through a shell or other object. Soon, however, this awl or splint was inserted in the bottom of a stick, the stick held between the hands and the palms of the hands rubbed back and forth to twirl it. The process was speeded up greatly, however, when the thong drill was discovered: A two-foot thong was used with a little stick tied at each end so that it could be gripped easily with the hands, the thong was wrapped once round the spindle, the spindle set upright with its upper end fitting into a little socket of wood which was held in the mouth; by pressing down with his mouth and pulling the thong back and forth the spindle was twirled to drill the hole. Then came the bow drill which was almost identical with the fire-by-friction outfit described in Chapter VI except that a splint of bone or hard rock was inserted in the bottom of the spindle with which to do the drilling.

All of these methods, however, were slow, tedious and inefficient as compared to the *pump drill* shown in Figure 168 which is a rig that every camper should know. It has been used these many years by pioneers and other people in out-of-the-way places, and is still used by the Pueblo Indian artists in making their jewelry, and indeed by many present-day craftsmen. It is uncertain whether or not this drill was known to the Indians before it was introduced from Europe.

The spindle is about fifteen inches long and three-quarters of an inch in diameter, in the bottom of which a nail is driven, the head of which is cut off and the end filed to a point. Or, if you want to do it strictly in the primitive way, drill a hole in the bottom of the spindle and insert the splint of a deer's leg. At the top of the drill a hole is bored through which the thong is inserted. The cross-piece shaped as in A is about eight inches long with a hole in it large enough so that the spindle will slip freely through it. The piece shown at B is merely a two-inch section sawed from a four-inch log with a hole drilled in the center of such size that the spindle will fit so snugly into it that it cannot move. A little glue may be used to hold it fast. In the city a square block may be used instead of the round section of a log, secured by sawing off a four-inch piece of a two-by-four.

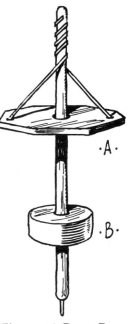

Figure 168. PUMP DRILL

With the rig set as in 168, press the cross-piece downward and the spindle will revolve. When the thong has unwound it will immediately start winding again, pulling the cross-piece up, whereupon it is again pushed down and so the process goes on endlessly. The pump drill operates with no effort at all and will drill holes through shells, bone, hardwood, and softer metal.

WOODCRAFT SANDPAPER

We marvel at the finished knifemanship of the Woods Indian—the remarkably smooth surfaces on his long pipestem, his ladle, his war club, and his bow. How does he get this perfect smoothness with no sandpaper to help him? And what can we use for sandpaper in the woods? It's really too simple to record: The Indian puts a handful of sand on a piece of buckskin and rubs the sand on the wood! For the finishing stages, he selects fine sand and then polishes with buckskin alone. Coarse cloth may be substituted for buckskin but it should be remembered that leather is a first-class polishing agent.

But the red folks have yet another way—rubbing the wood with the rough sandpaper-like stalks of *horsetail* or *scouring rush* (*Equisetum*), which, because of the generous supply of silica within them, bite into the wood, wear it down, and smooth it up as a good abrasive should.

The talented red carpenters of the Northwest Coast who were also fishermen *par excellence* used shark-skin in sanding their boards, this in addition to the materials named above.

Levels

A saucer of water is the backwoodsman's level. Place it on the surface in question and the water will tell the story. In leveling the ground, lay a board on the ground and put the saucer of water on it.

Woodcraft Pins

For pins use the thorns of *thorn-apple* or *honey-locust.* The old squaw of the woods was sure to have a buckskin bag containing a good supply of these, with which to pin up the children's clothing to keep them warm in winter, and in fact to serve all of the many needs for which pins are used in this present day with its countless conveniences that go to make life easy.

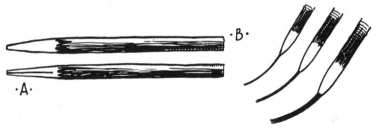

Figure 169. Twig Pens

Twig Pens

Elsworth Jaeger suggests this interesting method of making lettering pens from materials found in the woods. Cut some hardwood twigs the size of a lead pencil, split the end with a wide notch as shown in A, Figure 169, trim the sides down to the width of the line desired, and then thin the top and bottom down as seen in B. Square up the end and the pen is ready to use. An assortment of these pens should be made with points of various widths so that lines of any size can be made. These are good sign-painting pens.

Quill Pens.—See Chapter XXI.

SUBSTITUTES FOR CORKS

Use a corncob. It's been the "cork" of the North American continent for these many centuries.

WAR CLUBS

Of what use are they? None at all, not even to the Indians! Nor have they been of much practical value to the Indians these countless years, not since the bow and arrow were developed to relegate them largely to the limbo of forgotten time. But they are fun nevertheless! —fun for you and me who like to whittle in the rugged woodsy way, and fun for the Redmen of every tribe who continue to make them in the true, ancient way of their fathers, and to carry them as symbolic ornaments in their dances and ceremonies after the manner of those old heroes who have crossed the Great Divide.

There are two main types of wooden *pogamoggans:* The round-ball type shown in A, Figure 170, typical at once of the Plains and the Timber folk, used almost universally throughout the East, North and West, and still carried by the proud old Redmen who love to live over in the dance the glories of the past. The *musket-shaped club* seen in J is widely used by the Sioux and related Plains tribes, and is also popular among the Chippewas of the northern woods.

Ball-Shaped Clubs.—This is the better of the two types, so let us tackle it, even though it is at once the harder to make. For use in our shows and dances today we can fake these clubs from softwood such as cedar or basswood, but let us first see how the authentic ones can be made in Indian fashion, for no one would want to make an imitation unless he had to. To make a beautiful war club that would have served magnificently in the ancient days of hand-to-hand fighting, the wood to use is *hard maple* or *birch*, preferably the former—the Chippewas would use nothing else if they could get maple. Find a maple stump that spreads out into large roots at the surface of the ground as in B, Figure 170. The wood is not only tough here at ground level but the grain swings out to conform to the curve of the bark and thus to the shape of the club, and further, the bird's-eye formation produces a beautiful ball. Saw or chop out the section indicated by the dotted line in B. If this type of a stump cannot be found, drop a maple or birch six inches in diameter and cut off an eighteen-inch length from it near the ground.

Square up the piece of wood to the dimensions shown in C and D, 3 by 4½ by 18 inches. Draw the shape of the war club on the sides of this as shown and then saw or chop out along the dotted lines—it is hard work to whittle out a maple club when one does not have a saw with which to shape it up roughly. With the block so cut out, proceed to whittle the club to the shape shown in E, F, and G, Figure 170, which drawings show the various views of it. Try to get the ball as nearly perfect in roundness as possible with the knife, although a few irregularities will not matter because this is a hand-made, primitive instrument; then use a wood rasp if you have it to rub off any shoulders or projections that the knife may have left. Finish by scraping it with a piece of broken glass and smoothing it all up with sandpaper. It is much easier to whittle the club when it is green but we must remember that we cannot smooth it up with glass or sandpaper until it has dried out. The Indian would shape it up roughly and then let it dry for a couple of weeks before finishing it.

Now to ornament it: Note the decoration on the ancient club in A, made by a fine old Indian now with his fathers. There is a fish indicated on the top of the handle with his carved head resting on the ball. Such carving is not essential, but two things *are* important: The ball must be polished until it shines and a simple design must be applied to the handle with a hot wire, using the method described at the beginning of this chapter under "Burnt Etching." *Avoid all markings on the ball and all polish on the handle*—the shining ball should stand out in contrast to the handle. To polish the ball, rub linseed oil into it and brush it with a rough cloth, rub in more oil and polish again, keeping this up until it will shine no brighter. Varnish or paint should be avoided. The drawings show the type of simple geometric design to use on the handle. A tuft of fluffies may be attached to the end of the handle.

To imitate these clubs from softwood, use basswood or white cedar, making the ball and handle separately, and joining them together as in H, Figure 170. Whittle the end of the handle to the exact shape of the ball and attach by two long screws or dowling pins. If screws are used, countersink them and glue wooden plugs in the holes. If there is a little space showing between the handle and

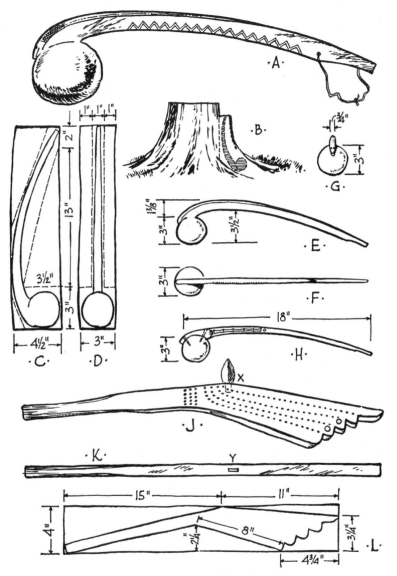

Figure 170. INDIAN WAR CLUBS

the ball, it may be filled in with plastic wood. Perhaps an old wooden ball can be found such as a croquet ball or a ten-pin ball.

Musket-shaped War Club.—This *pogamoggan*, so widely used among various Indian tribes, is called the musket-club because it resembles a rifle stock. We see it in J, Figure 170, and the method of construction is obvious from K and L. On a one-inch board of soft wood four inches wide and twenty-six inches long, draw the

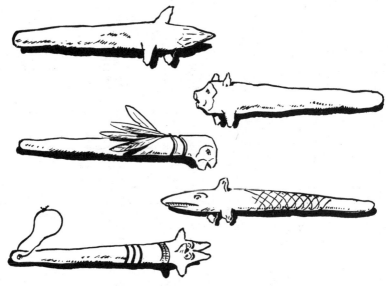

Figure 171. CARVED CLUBS FROM ROOTS

outline of the club as in L, and saw it out. The spear point seen at *x* in J is made from an extra piece of wood and glued in the hole shown at *y* in K. In the old days this was made from flint shaped like an arrowhead or spear point, and in more recent years, from metal and old knife blades. Often one sees a war club among the Indians to this day with a sharply pointed stone thus inserted. In whittling the point from wood, make it an inch and a half wide and about three inches long.

Decorate the war club by etching it with a hot wire or awl, or by fire coloration, as described earlier in this chapter.

Mauls and Sledge Hammers.—Frequently the Indians made vicious looking clubs by using a burl for the knob at the end, but these were used as *mauls* or *sledge hammers* rather than war clubs, although they could well have done service in time of war.

Carved Clubs from Roots.—The interesting clubs shown in Figure 171, although scarcely of the traditional Indian pattern, are nevertheless delightful whittling projects. They are made from small saplings about two inches in diameter, cut off just below the ground so as to utilize the roots for legs, ears, noses, etc. *Blue beech* is probably the best wood for this purpose and the usual custom is to leave the smooth bark on except at the carved end, adding to its attractiveness by soaking it with linseed oil and rubbing it strenuously with a rough cloth. Scrape the ground away from the roots of the sapling and cut it beneath the surface, leaving the roots projecting, and then study it to see what kind of a creature you can create—use your imagination!

Other Indian War Clubs.—See Chapter XVIII, "Rawhide," and Chapter XXIV, "Totem Poles."

Fungus Pictures

As the summer camping season nears its close, go a-foraging in the woods for a large bracket fungus such as that in Figure 172, growing on the trunk of a tree near the ground or on an old fallen log. Place your handkerchief beneath as you pry it loose and keep it wrapped until you get back to camp, because the *slightest mark or indentation on the light-colored bottom surface will remain permanently*. Saw off square the back side of the fungus, that is, the side that was attached to the tree, so that it will sit flat on the table. Now with an awl, ice-pick, pointed twig, or even a pencil, draw any picture that you want on the light undersurface of the fungus. Each mark shows brown and is permanently fixed for all time to come. Scenes of the camp-site can be so drawn to serve as a reminder of happy days when placed on the mantel at home, or records of honors received and achievements attained in camp can be thus recorded in a most appropriate and woodsy fashion. All of the dark areas of the fungus around the top and back side should be well shellacked with repeated coats, but the shellacking should not be carried down on to the light surface containing the picture.

Fungus Candle-Holder.—Find a wide bracket fungus, one that extends out from the tree several inches. Hunt up an old slab with rough, mossy bark and saw off a section as seen in D, Figure 172, or chop out a board that is rough and knotty. Saw off the back side

of the fungus as indicated in B and cut away the bark of the slab
to the shape of the fungus so as to offer a flat surface on which to
attach it, as in D and E. A couple of screws or a nail or two will hold
the fungus fast. With a jackknife cut a hole an inch wide in the
top shelf of the fungus and insert the candle as shown. If the bark

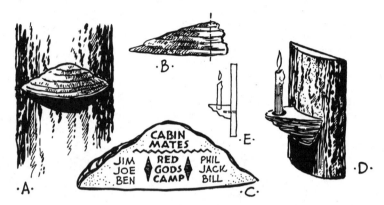

Figure 172. Uses of Fungus

of the slab is rough and mossy the fungus will blend into it to make
a delightful candle-holder for the wall of a cabin.

Whistles

We make them from basswood or willow with a bark covering,
from elderberry with its large hollow center, or from cane or bamboo.

Basswood or Willow Whistles.—Cut a green branch of basswood
or willow three-quarters of an inch in diameter and four to six
inches long. Bevel the mouth end on the lower side as seen at x in A,
Figure 173, and cut the notch y on the upper side about an inch or
a little less from the mouth end. Now pound the bark gently with a
stick or roll it between two boards and presently the bark will
loosen enough so that it can be slipped off. Now whittle the wood
center to the shape shown in B, flattening the top at the mouth end
enough so that the air can get through when it is blown. Slip the
wooden core back into the bark and the whistle is ready to use, as in C.

If you will make the section at z longer, extending it almost the
entire length of the whistle, and then cut a little hole through the
bark as seen at y in D, you will have a *two-tone whistle*—by blowing

in it with the hole at y open we get one tone, and by placing the finger over the hole we get another.

"Clean as a whistle!" How did the old saying originate? You will know when first you slip off the basswood bark to reveal the matchless whiteness and purity of the wood beneath.

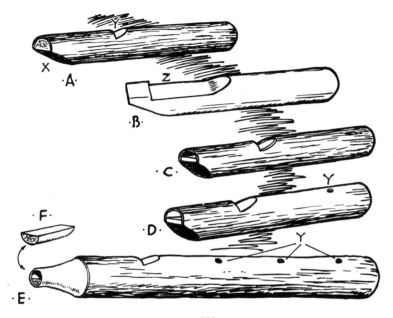

Figure 173. WHISTLES

Elderberry Whistles.—The large pithy center in an elderberry branch can easily be pushed out with the wire and the inside further cleaned out with a long pointed instrument to make a hole large enough for the whistle. Since the shell of this whistle is of wood it is more substantial and enduring than those of basswood or willow with only a bark covering over the excavated sections. We see such a whistle in E, Figure 173. The elderberry stick should be an inch in diameter and six or more inches in length. Whittle the mouth end down small enough so that it is of a convenient size and then whittle a plug of basswood or other soft wood as seen at F to be inserted in the hole at the mouth end. Cut the notch as shown, drill one or more holes along the top as seen at y and plug up the far end. By manipulating the fingers over the holes at y we can produce several different tones.

Cane and Bamboo Whistles.—From a piece of cane or bamboo not over an inch in diameter we can make an excellent whistle fashioned in the same way as the elderberry one. A joint or node of the bamboo closes the far end and a wooden plug as at F is inserted in the mouth end. Bamboo lends itself beautifully to the making of whistles of several tones and can in fact be fashioned into an instrument resembling a flute. If it is of ordinary whistle size drill two or three small holes on the top side near the end as described for the elderberry whistle—by manipulating the fingers over these, different tones can be produced. To make a kind of flute, use a piece of bamboo at least a foot in length and burn out all the joints except the one used to close the end, by pushing a hot rod into the tube and against the partitions. Then turn it into a whistle as already described and drill a series of six or eight holes spaced an inch apart along the top side. Manipulate the fingers over these to obtain the different tones.

Squirt-Guns, Pea-Shooters and Blowguns

In another book, *Primitive and Pioneer Sports,* I devoted an entire chapter to the subject of how to make and use the long blowgun of the Cherokee Indian and its arrows feathered with thistledown, and also offered suggestions for the use of modern and easily obtained substitutes for this picturesque weapon. Those who are interested in this appealing sport will find the details there.

For small *squirt-guns* and *pea-shooters* the children of the woods these countless years have used branches of *elderberry*. When the large pithy center is cleaned out by pushing a wire through, we have a hollow tube made to order for the purpose. A guncleaner may be used to smooth up the interior. Beans, peas, pebbles or even small darts made of splints of wood may be shot through these, but the darts need a little wadding at one end to catch the air, such as a little cotton or a piece of cork into which the butt end of the dart is thrust. A sudden puff zips it out while a long steady blow floats it lazily.

Camp Candlesticks

The significant items for the camper in Figure 174 are the candlesticks shown in A, B and C, which are of the type used when camping

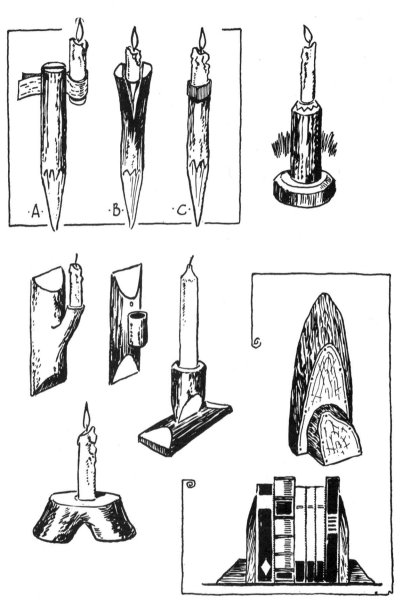

Figure 174. CANDLESTICKS AND BOOKENDS

in a tent. In A the peg is split, a strip of birch-bark bent around the candle and then inserted in the split. This is an ancient and widely used arrangement but becomes dangerous when the candle burns low because birch-bark is extremely inflammable, and so it is better to remove the short stub of candle from the bark and insert it in the split, as shown in B. The handiest and safest arrangement of all, however, is to cut a peg of the size of the candle, set the candle on top, and then wrap an inch strip of *adhesive tape* around to hold the two together as seen in C. All of the sticks have pointed bottoms to thrust into the ground.

A candlestick of excellent breeding in pioneer circles is a *potato* with a hole cut in it to receive the candle. Among coast-wise dwellers a large *cork* from a fish net does similar duty, and *shells* of many shapes are utilized. And of course there are always bottles with openings of suitable size to grip the candle.

The other candlesticks, match-holders and bookends in Figure 174 are merely camp handicraft ideas which would be appropriate in cabins and which are simple projects for those who like to make things from rough materials. This display could be expanded to cover many pages but once started at it no one would have trouble in figuring out scores of useful gadgets on this order to make during his odd moments.

Sun Goggles

From the blinding brightness of the far northern ice fields come these intriguing goggles for protecting the eyes from the glare of the sun. Indispensable they are in that far-off vivid land with its six months of shining day made overbright by the reflection from the whiteness of the eternal snow. Snow blindness is common enough at best and were it not for these goggles eyesight would be rare indeed among those who call the ice fields home.

But of what use are they to us?—especially in this day of smoked and tinted sunglasses? An overbright sun is definitely harmful to the eyes and one who is living in the open, either on snow or water, should have protection. These wooden goggles are better than sunglasses, better for the eyes and more efficient in keeping out the glare. There is no reflection or penetration of light from the sides. They fit tight, do not brush off in the woods, and do not break. Furthermore, they can be made in the woods and sunglasses cannot. When our smoked glasses break in the bush, wooden goggles are the only possible resort. Tradition has associated these goggles with the snow fields—in fact they are usually called snow goggles—but they are equally effective on the water and are to be recommended for use by the paddler and fisherman.

While the snow goggles of the Eskimo and the Northern Indian were made in a great variety of styles,* each individual fashioning his own according to his own taste and taking much pride in his craftsmanship, all are of two general types, those made of one piece as in A, Figure 175, and those made of two pieces as in F. Let us first describe those made of one piece:

Softwood makes an easy job of it but it will pay to spend a little extra time to produce a more substantial pair from harder woods of close grain such as *beech, ash,* or *birch.* Cut out a block 1⅛ by 1⅝ by 6 inches in size as shown in C, being sure that the wood is straight-grained and clear, free from knots or blemishes. Cut to these dimensions, the block will be amply large so that it can be trimmed down to fit your face. Much grief will be saved if we cut out a pattern from cardboard to the curve of the forehead just at the level of the eyebrows. Place this pattern on the edge of the block of wood, mark the curved line, and then cut out the curved section as shown in C. Now whittle out the bridge for the nose by laying the block over the eyes at frequent intervals, fitting and whittling until the wood fits snugly. Next we must gouge out the hollows for the eyes as seen in D, using a gouge, crooked knife (page 61), or ordinary jackknife. Here again we fit the goggles to the eyes repeatedly to guide us in our work, remembering that the goggles will be more comfortable if ample room is provided for the eyes--at its center the hollow should be a full half inch deep. We may now complete the goggles by cutting away the outside wood as indicated by the dotted lines in E to produce a thin shell. Before thinning down the shell too much it is well to cut the eye slits with the point of a sharp pocketknife, thus enabling us to determine how thick the wood is so that we can intelligently complete the thinning-down process. If made of hardwood the shell directly over the eyes can be thinned down to a sixteenth of an inch, but if the wood is soft and fragile, it should remain at nearly an eighth of an inch in thickness. Note in B that

* See *Report of the United States National Museum* for 1894, pages 281 to 306. (Washington: Government Printing Office.)

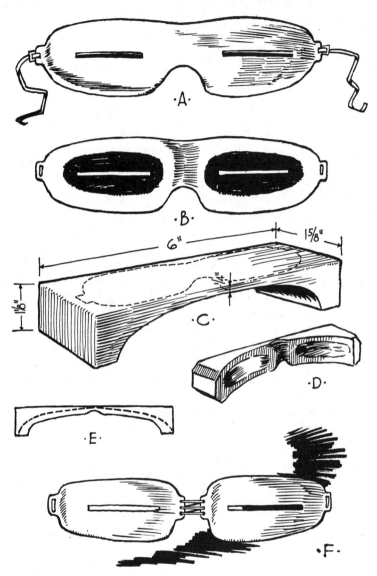

Figure 175. SUN GOGGLES FROM THE FAR-NORTHERN ICE FIELDS

there are holes at the ends of the goggles to receive the buckskin thongs or strings with which the goggles are tied on.

To complete the job in Eskimo fashion paint the inside of the goggles and also the edges of the slits with black paint.

The natives of the northern ice fields often used visors in addition to sun goggles and frequently combined the two, so constructing the goggles that there was a projection from the top edge for about an inch. For use on the water this is scarcely necessary.

The goggles made of two pieces shown in F have certain advantages over those we have just described. They are easier to carry because they fold up to fit conveniently in the pocket, and they are also easier to make. They can be fashioned from a five-eighths-inch board by whittling and fitting until they conform to the contour of the forehead and eyes. The pieces are attached together with a buckskin thong at the bridge of the nose.

LACROSSE STICKS

Wherever the early explorers journeyed in the woodlands, plains or mountains they found the Indians playing a strenuous, fighting ball game with rackets resembling somewhat a tennis racket. The French adventurers called it *"la crosse"* because of the shape of the racket. That this game had merit and playing value is proven by the fact that we have taken it over ourselves and are playing it today as a college sport, using a racket copied after that of the Iroquois.

This is a challenging camp game because we can make the rackets and the balls from materials found in the woods. If all we want to do is to throw together a lacrosse stick in the shortest possible time, we can cut a crotched stick similar to that shown in E, twenty inches long below the crotch, and form the net between the prongs by running heavy wrapping cord across as illustrated. This will last for a game or two but is scarcely true to the Indian pattern. Better make a good one that will last for several years:

While the lacrosse sticks vary in shape as we go from tribe to tribe they fall for the most part into four general types shown in A, B, C and D, Figure 176. That at A is from the Chippewas, B from the Cherokees, C from the Choctaws, and D from the Iroquois.

The Chippewa stick in A has a thirty-inch handle as indicated, the circular end measuring four inches in diameter, inside measurement. Secure a stick of *ash* if possible, otherwise *hickory* or any strong, pliable wood, cutting it forty-eight inches long. While a branch may be used it is better to cut the stick out of a log. The handle is one inch in diameter throughout its thirty-inch length except that it widens out to an inch and a quarter just below the beginning of the bend to form the racket—this becomes obvious from the diagram of the handle in F. The remaining eighteen inches of the stick is thinned

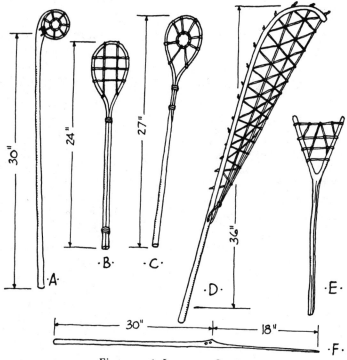

Figure 176. Lacrosse Sticks

down to a thickness of about three-eighths inch but retains its full width of one inch. After the green wood has been soaked for a few hours in water, the thinned-down end is bent to form the circle and is lashed to the main stick as shown in A, Figure 176, by means of a rawhide thong run through two holes cut for the purpose as indicated in F. The Chippewas used buckskin thongs to form the net illustrated in A, run through holes drilled through the side of the racket, but heavy wrapping cord makes a good substitute.

The Cherokees (Smoky Mountain) and the neighboring tribes used a much smaller lacrosse stick constructed as shown in B. It measures about twenty-four inches over all and is made from a slender stick split in half to form a flat surface which is then bent at its middle to form the circular racket, the two ends being lashed together to form the handle. The construction of the Choctow stick in C is obvious at a glance—the stick is well soaked in water and then bent around a pole to form the circular end.

Our modern lacrosse sticks are modeled after the Iroquois type shown in D. These Iroquois sticks are from thirty to thirty-six inches in length and are bent to a crook on the end as shown. The net extends from the bent end down the handle for about two-thirds of its length. The outer cord is a heavy one and is installed first, then the two other lengthwise thongs of lighter string are tied in place, and lastly the crosswise strings are woven back and forth as shown, being tied firmly to the outer cord and to the stick.

All of these styles of lacrosse sticks have a racket measuring about four inches across or a trifle more, with the exception of the Iroquois style which measures about eight inches at its widest point. The nets of all are loose enough so as to sag sufficiently to form a shallow pocket in which to catch the ball.

The rules for playing lacrosse can be found in many games books.

Lacrosse Balls.—The northern Woodland Indians usually make their lacrosse balls out of white cedar with a hole drilled through the center to lighten the weight. These measure about two-and-one-half inches in diameter and are easy to whittle out in that they do not need to be perfectly round. Light as these cedar balls are, however, there is enough of an element of danger in their use to make it unwise to play this strenous game with them. Better to make the ball out of buckskin or other soft leather, stuffing it with hay or hair. The quickest method, and one that will produce as serviceable a ball as any, is to make a little bag out of soft leather and stuff it with grass or hair, using the puckering string at the opening to close it. Whatever the method used the size of the ball should measure from two-and-one-half to three inches in diameter unless we are using the small Cherokee racket, in which case the ball would measure an inch-and-one-half to two inches. Discarded tennis balls that have gone dead are much used for lacrosse.

WOODSY FURNITURE AND CAMP FIXINGS

THERE IS BUT ONE RULE—it must *belong*, must *blend*, must *fit the setting*, whether it be cabin, outdoor kitchen, bench, stool or whatnot in the woods. That which is wholly in order in the city may raise its distressing head with consummate ugliness in the wilds. And that which melts into one scene as though nature grew it there may be strikingly incongruous in another outdoor setting. To have the feel of belonging, it must be of material native to the setting and must be unobtrusively simple. With too much of man's cunning in it, the natural surroundings rebel to throw it out of focus.

Beyond that of naturalness, there are no laws to prescribe the types, no formulas to govern the styles of camp fixings. Each camper is a law unto himself, guided only by the opportunities of the materials at hand. Happily so, for monotony of appearance is thus avoided. And this being the case there is no brief word that will be adequate in one short chapter and volumes would be required to indicate the possibilities.

And so just a wrinkle or two by way of suggestion, with the thought in mind always that we fashion only that which is essential when on the trail, and think in terms of simple furniture and fixings with pleasing lines only in the more permanent camps.

AROUND A TEMPORARY CAMP

Time is precious if we're only going to stay on the spot for a few days, too precious to waste building a lot of conveniences. A log or a stump is a good enough seat and a poncho on the ground a first-class dining table. We'll need a few *pegs* to hang things on—coats, hats, creels, packs, kettles, etc.—and if a tree with stumps of branches protruding is not close at hand, drive some pegs in the nearest live tree trunk as was done· at A, Figure 177. This is accomplished by sharpening the peg wedge shape, striking the ax in the tree vertically, and then driving the peg in the crack just created. It will drive in easily

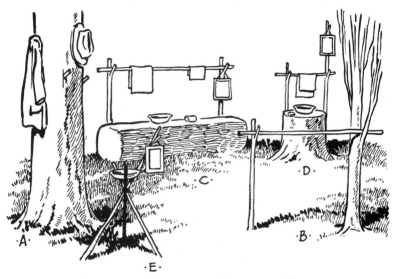

Figure 177. FIXINGS FOR A TEMPORARY CAMP

and hold solidly under a heavy load. A small vertical cut like this heals very quickly and does the tree no damage at all, *provided you pull the peg out before leaving.* In lieu of pegs, a hanging and drying pole may be erected horizontally as at B.

The lake or river is good enough for anybody to wash in, but if you figure on staying a while and insist on shaving, rig up a washstand from a stump or a log as shown in C and D in Figure 177, or arrange a tripod as in E. The two shorter poles of the tripod are thirty inches long. Notches are cut to catch the edges of the washbasin.

Beds are described in Part 1, Chapter V, "Beds and Duffel," and *caches* in Chapter IX.

For the Pots and Dishes

Dishes should be spread out after they are washed, preferably in the sun, and not stacked up. With only three or four in the party the arrangement shown in A, Figure 178, will suffice. Built near the camp-fire the bench does service as a kitchen table while cooking and as a drying rack for the dishes afterwards, the plates being leaned

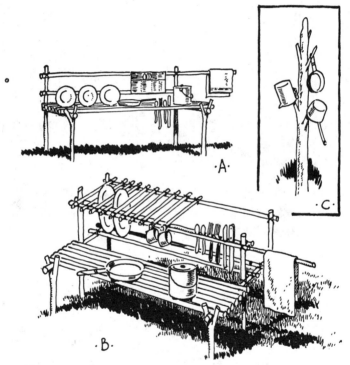

Figure 178. Racks and Hangers for the Pots and Dishes

against the back pole, and the silverware either slipped down between the poles of the bench as illustrated or kept in a canvas case attached to the back pole. These canvas cases are handy—there is a compartment each, for knives, forks, spoons, and serving spoons, and two grommet holes at the top edge permit us to hang it as shown; when moving it folds and rolls up to fit in the cooking-outfit bag, and so the silverware is always assembled and never scattered.

If there are many in the party as in a pioneer unit of an organized camp, the arrangement shown in B, often used in Girl Scout camps, is better. These racks can be made to hold any number of dishes and the bench in front is utilized as a cooking table, dish-washing shelf, and a convenient place for the pans. A slab is often built into these racks as a support for the dishes but the use of two poles as in the illustration is at once more dependable and sanitary.

In a shifting camp the stubs of branches on a dead tree will hold the pots and pans as shown in C, and if such is not handy, pegs may be driven in a nearby tree as described in the preceding section of this chapter.

PACKING BOXES OR BARREL STAVES

The first stage of furniture making that a boy experiences is the rigging up of small packing boxes for seats and tables. These are not to be scoffed at in woodcraft because a little square packing box of

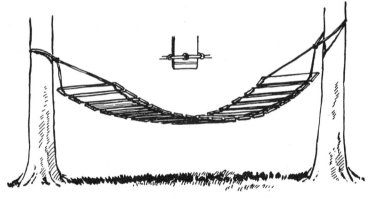

Figure 179. BARREL-STAVE HAMMOCK

a size suitable for a low chair, with a back of packing-box lumber nailed on at an angle, can be made delightfully appropriate for a den or cabin *by painting Indian symbols and totems on its four sides and back.* An assortment of these, all decorated differently, will add color aplenty of the proper type to a meeting room for outdoor-minded folks. They are better in such rooms, however, than in the woods. Volumes have been written on making packing-box furniture so none of our precious space can be addressed to the details here.

The important thing to remember is to keep the articles exceedingly simple and to decorate them with symbols and totems true in every detail to the Indian and backwoods patterns.

Barrel staves, too, are in the same class with packing boxes for the fashioning of crude furniture. As seats for benches their chief recommendation is that they are not only appropriate in size and shape but provide a springiness designed to add comfort to the seat. If too long for the purpose, they are nailed to the bottom and back of the bench and then sawed to length afterward.

Don't forget the *barrel-stave hammock* of the pioneers, so thoroughly appropriate when suspended between two trees near a simple cabin in the woods. Figure 179 shows it. A hole is drilled through the end of each stave as shown, and two braided cotton ropes run through, one from above and the other from below, and knotted in the space between the slabs to prevent them from sliding out of place.

Slab Stools and Benches

The shortest trail to camp seats is a trip to the nearest sawmill for some discarded slabs. All that is needed to convert them into stools and benches is to bore holes in the bottom and drive in round branches for legs. Simple, rugged, picturesque, long used by the pioneers, these are most appropriate camp seats, appropriate alike out-of-doors, in a cabin by a fireplace, or in a city meeting room or den where outdoor atmosphere is in order. Move past the packing-box and barrel-stave stage, and use slabs to create stools that look right in the woods. You can make a half dozen of these in a couple of hours.

The only tools we need are an ax and an inch-and-a-quarter auger as seen at M in Figure 180. Pick out a good thick slab a foot in width and saw off about fifteen inches of it. Bore four holes with the auger as seen in A, Figure 180, or if you can find a slab with a distinct taper, wider at one end than the other, drill three holes as in B, to make a three-legged stool. For the legs use hardwood branches an inch and a half to two inches in diameter. Trim the leg down as in E to fit the hole, split the end and drive in place, then cut off the protruding end and drive a hardwood wedge in the split. Remember that green wood will shrink as it dries to loosen the leg and so if we would make a sturdy bench that will stand up for years, the legs must be of seasoned stuff. Made of green wood, a new wedge will have to be inserted in a month or so.

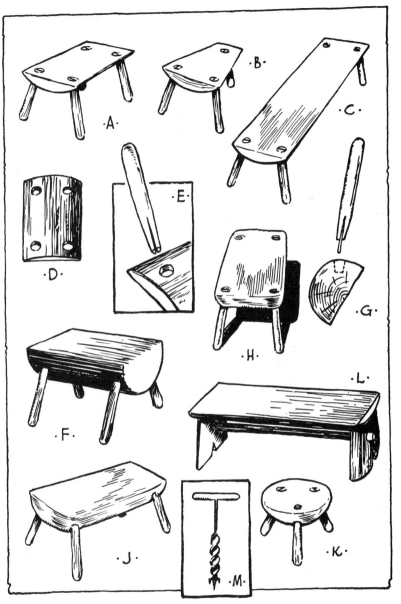

Figure 180. SLAB STOOLS AND BENCHES

If we can find an unusually thick slab the thing to do is to use a *blind wedge* as illustrated in G, to form the stool shown in F. To do this bore the hole about two-thirds of the way through the slab, split the end of the leg, and insert the wedge before it is driven in; the wedge will be forced deep into the leg as it strikes the end of the bore. This method is much to be preferred if the wood is green because the leg can be driven in farther after it dries.

If no sawmill slabs are to be had we shall have to split a one-foot log in two. Saw the log into fourteen or fifteen-inch sections before splitting it because it is easier to split chunks than long logs. The stool in F was made in this way.

Leave the bark on the slab and legs unless you want a particularly finished stool to use in a cabin. In that case the slab can be peeled and the lower part of it smoothed off to make the trim stool shown in H. In J we have a stool made by rounding off the ends of a thick slab to a pleasing curve.

The characteristic three-legged stool of the pioneers seen at K is made by cutting a slab to a roughly circular shape and trimming off the bottom.

The usual height of stools and chairs is eighteen inches, the customary procedure being to make them a little higher than that and then saw off the legs after they are completed.

Log Benches

For outside seats around a woodland camp, logs are in a class all their own—massive and sturdy, they radiate the strength and stamina of the forests and the ruggedness of its dwellers. Figure 187 shows an assortment from logs and half-logs. The tops of the full logs are hewed to a flat surface and the half-logs are produced by splitting, both the hewing and the splitting processes being described in Chapter VIII, "Axmanship." Massive logs may be cut out to form a seat and back as in E and F, and half-logs may rest on crosswise poles or rocks to give them elevation as in G.*

Wherever possible add the touch of color, the bit of decorative design, to high light the bench with interest and attractiveness. The round ends of logs lend themselves admirably to painted decorations,

---

* For a description of many types of orthodox log benches and trail seats, and also of outdoor tables, see A. H. Good, *Park and Recreation Structures*, Part II (Washington: Government Printing Office, 1938).

Figure 181. A Log Seat

Figure 182. An "Alligator" Bench Using Branches for Legs

as seen in B, C, D and E, Figure 187, and in Figure 181. The Indian's matchless wealth in decorative design will offer countless types of ornamentation that blend with the woodland background as though to the manner born. Avoid all modern symbols and all realistic pictures.

The top or upper section of a fallen tree will have many protruding branches which can be cut off so as to form natural legs for a bench, as in the case of the one shown in Figure 182. A head can be carved on the end of such a log to create an "alligator" or "crocodile," or similar short-legged creature. Study the branches on the log and use your imagination to figure out the possibilities.

Backs may be constructed for logs that lie flat on the ground by driving the upright poles in the ground as indicated in B, or nailing them on the flattened back side of the log as in C.

Bizarre Benches of Cedar

White cedar does queer things. It is the acrobat among the trees. It twists and turns, ties itself up in knots, and distorts itself generally in getting into all sorts of shapes and positions unbecoming for a tree. Out in the open its behavior is usually quite proper but back in the tangle of the cedar swamp it assumes its circus role and becomes a contortionist. And in doing so it leads right into the hands of those who like to make odd-looking benches.

Head into the cedar swamp and take your imagination along. Study every bent and twisted tree with a chair or seat in mind and let your imagination run riot. Soon you will have cut down the makings for as bizarre and grotesque a set of benches as was ever made. But not all of them will be weird, for some will have unusually graceful curves and pleasing lines.

In every cedar swamp there are sure to be many cedars whose trunks lie flat on the ground for a number of feet before swinging up, and extending upward from these trunks will be branches; by cutting such a tree and severing the branches a few feet above the trunk, and then turning the whole affair upside down, the branches become the legs of a bench. That is the way the bench shown in Figure 191 was made—in its natural state the top of the bench rested on the ground and what now are legs were branches growing upward. All that was needed to make a bench of it was to build on the seat.

And likewise the bench shown in Figure 189 was made from a prostrate cedar tree with its branches turned into legs. By carving

Figure 183. CEDAR-ROOT CHAIR

Figure 184. CEDAR-ROOT CHAIR

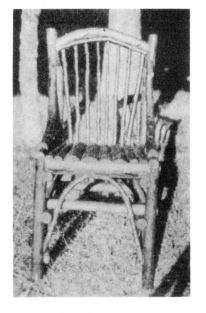

Figure 185. WHITE-CEDAR CHAIR

Photographs taken at Camp Fairwood

Figure 186. A STUMP SEAT

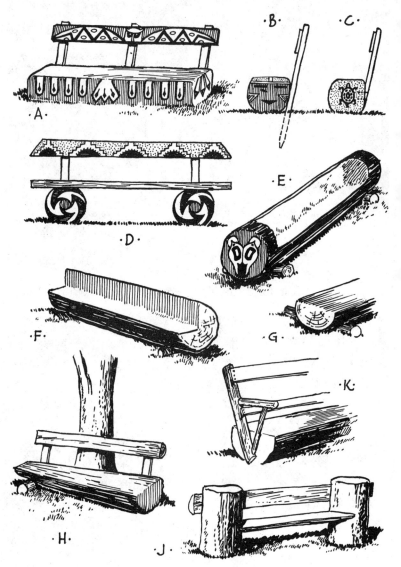

Figure 187. LOG BENCHES

Figure 188. A "Horse" Found in the Cedar Swamp

Photographs taken at Camp Fairwood

Figure 189. Bizarre Bench from a Cedar Root

a head on one end of it the bench became a prehistoric monster of some indescribable sort.

And believe it or not the *horse* shown in Figure 188 is a natural—all that we did to it was to carve the eyes and add the platform on which to sit. His head was the root and his legs were the saplings growing upward.

Pleasing curves such as those seen in Figure 190 are to be found no end in the cedar country.

One would hunt for many a long day before he would find the trees or roots that would exactly duplicate the benches shown in these photographs, but that is the interesting feature about making these bizarre seats—no two of them could conceivably be made alike for no two trees have the same twist and turn. The thing that makes these benches so intriguing is their grotesque quality, their extreme individuality. Some are graceful, some are fantastic, but all are compelling to the imagination. Don't try to duplicate the benches shown here—just wander among the cedars and let your imagination soar—the product will be something unique and all your own.

When it comes to *chairs* the cedar swamp is unusually generous. Ready-made frames for the backs of chairs like those in Figures 183 and 184 exist in countless array, all different and all interesting.

Get to know the cedar swamp. It's worth while not only for chairs and benches but for woodsy crafts in general.

Rustic Cabin Furniture

There is material for a book here and many a book covers it. It ranges all the way from the simplest to the finished, complex and fancy of the type manufactured by the furniture companies that specialize in the rustic. Just a couple of suggestions is all that a woodcraft book permits—and these appear in Figure 192.

Hat Tree.—Note the hat tree in F—it's just a pole with pegs driven in it and set in a spreading base of poles. Often we can find a sapling with branches so spaced that we can use the stubs of them for the pegs.

Wall Pegs.—We see them at D and E in Figure 192. That in D is made from a board or slab with pegs inserted in holes drilled for the purpose. The one in E is a sapling or a branch split in half so as to utilize an off-shooting branch for the peg.

Earlier in this chapter we saw that a peg can be driven into a tree

Figure 190. Utilizing the Natural Curves of White Cedar

Photographs taken at Camp Fairwood

Figure 191. Roots Like These Are Common in the Cedar Swamps

Figure 192. RUSTIC CABIN FURNITURE

by striking the tree vertically with the ax and then driving the peg in the slit thus created. This same process can be used on inside walls made of upright boards of softwood. The peg should be sharpened wedge shape, the ax struck into the board vertically and the peg driven into the crack. Most softwoods will take the peg without splitting and will grip it solidly.

Coat Hangers.—These can be fashioned in the woods in many ways but the suggestion offered in B, Figure 193, is the most practical and serviceable. Find a branch curved to the general shape of a coat hanger, drill a hole at its middle, and whittle the end of a forked stick so as to fit through it as illustrated. Then drill a small hole through the projecting section below the cross-piece and insert a tiny peg to hold it secure. A still simpler way is merely to tie a loop of wrapping cord to the middle of the cross-piece.

A quick and easy coat hanger can be extemporized by rolling up a newspaper and tying a loop of cord to its middle.

Broom Holders.—The broom holder which we see on the wall at G in Figure 192 is illustrated in detail at C in Figure 193. The back-

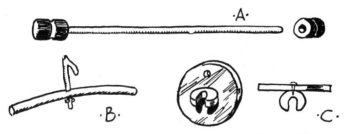

Figure 193. CURTAIN ROD, COAT HANGER AND BROOM HANGER

board consists of a circular section one inch thick sawed off from a five-inch log. The gadget which holds the broom is a two-inch section sawed off from a branch three inches in diameter, with a U-shaped notch cut in it just wide enough so that the broomstick can be slipped in. This is attached to the backboard with a screw or nail as illustrated. A hole should be drilled near the edge so that it can be hung on a nail and then the broom turned upside down and slipped in the notch as shown in G, Figure 192.

Curtain Hangers.—A simple and singularly appropriate curtain hanger for a cabin in the woods is shown in A, Figure 193. The end pieces are three inches long, sawed from a branch an inch and three-quarters in diameter. The bark is left on except for a groove a half inch wide whittled all the way around the piece at its middle. A three-quarter-inch hole is drilled in one end to receive the curtain rod which is three-quarters of an inch in diameter and whittled down at its end to slip easily into the hole. The half-inch groove is designed to fit over the bracket coming out from the wall to hold the rod up.

White birch can be used for the end pieces but a branch with a smooth dark-colored bark is more effective because the bark then contrasts with the white of the wood in the groove to give the curtain rod a more ornamental effect.

Settees.—They are limitless in shape and style, without law or pattern, governed only by the fancy of the maker and the size and shape of the poles at hand. As to wood, these are the more traditional ones—*white cedar, hickory, ironwood, white birch, poplar,* and *willow.* More rustic furniture is probably made from white cedar than from any other—it lends itself admirably to the purpose because it is pleasing to the eye whether with the bark on or off, is easy to work, and produces a settee at once substantial, enduring, light and easy to move. Hickory and ironwood produce excellent benches but are usually avoided by those who must work by hand because of their hardness. White birch is always popular owing to the attractiveness of its bark, and poplar has many followers also. Willow is sometimes used in making the fussy benches decorated with many curved twigs and shoots. But I'll take white cedar if it can be found.

As to shapes and styles, just a suggestion or two: In K, Figure 192, we have a massive yet simple bench. The variation in these simple benches is usually in the back and the arms at the end—all kinds of fancy backs can be made by fitting in small poles at various angles. In A, Figure 192, we have a more finished bench but at the same time a more difficult one to make. If the legs on this bench were vertical and the back legs continued up to form the end uprights of the back, it could be much more quickly tossed together. Note that the seat is made by split logs fitted together and pegged. This lends an unusually finished tone but is rare in home-made seats because of the time and skill it requires. Easier by far and equally as practical is to use small branches an inch to an inch and a half in diameter and nail them on crosswise of the seat as indicated in K.

Washstands.—When the washstand is placed just outside the cabin door as is so often the case in the woods, the ideal type of stand is shown in H, Figure 192. There is no solid top, no messy water-soaked boards—the slender poles that hold the washbasin permits spilled water to drop through to the ground freely. A leveled off spot on one of the heavy cross-poles at the ends will furnish a shelf for the soap.

In construction of this sort remember that it is important that the poles be seasoned or they will soon loosen to make the stand rickety.

Figure 194. A BED FROM OLD INNER TUBES

This can be forestalled to some extent by using blind wedges as described earlier in this chapter and illustrated at G in Figure 180.

Tables.—Two suggestions from the limitless possibilities for cabin tables appear at J and L in Figure 192. Table tops are best made from milled lumber but can be fashioned in true rustic fashion by splitting logs and fitting them together with pegs as in J, if one has the skill and patience.

An interesting stand can be made from a cluster of white-birch saplings growing from the same roots, cut as indicated in B, Figure 194. Gray birch also lends itself admirably to this type of construction because of the mass of wood to which the saplings are attached just below the surface of the ground, which can be flattened and leveled to receive the top. By cutting the saplings to proper length for legs, and adding a square or circular table top, a unique stand results.

Easy Chair.—Build it as in C, Figure 194, using canvas for the seat. Use brass-headed tacks if possible and attach the canvas temporarily to determine the proper sag for a comfortable seat before tacking it down solidly.

Inner-Tube Bunks.—Old inner tubes provide the material for a first-class substitute for springs in a cabin bunk. Cut the inner tubes into strips three inches wide, some long enough to extend lengthwise of the bunk and others shorter for the crosswise pieces. Using upholstering tacks if possible, nail on the lengthwise strips first, placing them close enough together so their edges almost touch. Then weave the crosswise strips in and out with the basket weave shown in Figure 194. By using strips from red inner tubes in one direction and white or gray tubes in the opposite direction, the checker board effect seen in Figure 194 is obtained. Plenty of blankets are needed underneath on a rubber cot.

Such inner-tube strips also make good seats for chairs and settees. For chairs, the strips should be narrower.

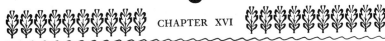
COUNCIL RINGS

VENING and the glamour of Council! The Redman's symbolism, the beauty of costume, the compulsion of atmosphere, the intrigue of ritual, the eternal youth of primitive dancing—all under the great canopy of the night, with the sweet incense of the things that grow and the thousand voices that only the Faithful hear and understand! And as its crowning glory, the sacred fire!

It was beside a fire in the woods that the first men found their gathering place. Throughout the ages humankind has formed in circles around warmth-giving, cheer-producing flames, and to this day the children of the wilds gravitate to the evening campfire as tired wanderers returning home.

The council is a glorified campfire, the council ring a glorified campfire circle. And it was the Indian who glorified it, with his matchless gift for simple and dignified, yet artistic, ceremony. From his tribal councils, his dancing circles, the council ring has evolved into one of the most picturesque institutions of camping and the outdoor way of living. Council rings there have been on this continent for—we know not how many centuries, but it remained for Ernest Thompson Seton first to borrow the idea from the Redman, adapt it, and introduce it in a way that was satisfying to the modern world. His adaptation is followed largely in the pages of this chapter.

The council ring is vital, most vital to camping. On the trail, the few may sit around the informal campfire, but in the permanent camp, particularly the organized camp with its many campers, the council ring is the central, the vital, spiritual organ. It is the hub

173

around which all things else move. It is the token, the symbol, of camp spirit. It is the very essence of we-ness, of self-regard, on the part of the camp, the thing that is central when thoughts turn to camp—not the council ring itself, of course, but what it signifies, for it represents tangibly and colorfully the vital, living spirit of the place.

It is joy—and happy memories; it is beauty—in·surroundings, in ceremonies, in ideals; it is friendship—warmth, life. All these, symbolized by one sacred spot, and that spot close to the things that grow, close to and of the earth-things!

But rather—it *can be* all these. They may be found lacking in a ring improperly made, they may be lost through inappropriate ceremonies and programs, they may fail to materialize through inadequate leadership. They are not made—they grow, and they thrive only in the proper soil.

Let us consider a few of the factors that help to make the council ring this lofty, vital element in camping.

What Happens in the Council Ring

It is the nightly gathering place, the evening rendezvous of all the clan. But it is no mere campfire circle, for tradition has hallowed the spot (witness that no one walks across it) and hallowed the ceremony with a certain amount of simple ritual. Within these traditional limitations, or rather glorified in these traditional ways, the usual types of campfire programs find their setting there. But there are other types that are not so common, being more or less unique to the ring, particularly in the way they are handled. Our task here is to describe the building of the ring, but we shall understand the why of it better if' first we know the purpose.

It is there that the story-teller finds the ideal setting for the unfolding of his art. Yet, an evening of stories is scarcely a council, even though in the council ring.

Council, from the activities standpoint, runs along two lines, with other minor additions to be recounted later: It is *games* and *Indian dancing*. It can concentrate on one to the exclusion of the other, or it can incorporate both.

Let's watch a play council in action. The ring is filled with eager faces, all eyes fixed on two in the center who are competing in a simple contest. The excitement is intense, the shouting loud—strange for so simple an event! One is defeated, and the chief asks for challengers for the winner. Challengers? There are scores! from whom one is quickly picked, and the event is repeated. Again one is defeated and the winner challenged, and so it goes, challenge after challenge, until there are no more and the champion is determined. Immediately the next game is started, and so on for better than an hour. There has been no lag, no dull moment—a hundred people have been thrilled. And yet *how simple the games were!* They could not have been otherwise or the council would not have moved so swiftly, and many would not have challenged had special skill been required. Simple, indeed, yet *how dramatic they seemed!* How eagerly the crowd watched and how they shouted! These same contests in another setting would seem dull and commonplace. That is a rare tribute to the council. Two factors explain it—the presence of the spectators and the fact that every spectator knows he can challenge. The gallery of spectators supplies the spark.

There is only one conclusion—here is the best approach to handling a large group in an active program when the space is limited. That means *it is the best approach to an evening of play in the woods, for the space is limited by the light of the campfire.*

But why tie-up this sort of thing with an Indian council ring? Verily, it comes from the Indian, from those ancient evening gatherings when the old folk recounted the tales of their youth and the youth competed one with another in challenging fashion.

What of the games and the techniques of leading such a play council? Temptation is strong to tell again of these many games and the dynamic type of leadership and showmanship required, but I have already set these forth in full in *Social Games for Recreation.* Those who are interested should consult Part II of that book.*

But the *second type of activity* characteristic of the council ring is of a loftier sort. Seldom did the Indians gather on occasions of importance without that glamorous spectacle, that most joyous type of expression—*dancing.* And so it is with many a camp council today, particularly for boys, for the dancing of the Redman is masculine, vigorous, and virile first of all, well suited for men and boys, but less so for women. The story of the Indian's dance-drama and the many dances that can be used today is material for a book in itself—we

* Bernard S. Mason and Elmer D. Mitchell, *Social Games for Recreation* (New York: A. S. Barnes & Co., 1935).

cannot go into it here, not even to paint the scintillating picture. There are many sources that can be consulted.*

Preliminary to the main body of the council-fire program, whatever its nature may be, is usually the opportunity for all who desire to recount their exploits and to tell of the things of interest they have seen recently on the trail and in the woods. Here, too, accomplishments are praised and honors awarded. And this again comes from those ancient Indian councils when the returning warriors portrayed in verbal drama the thrills of the warpath, when the aged ones full of honors told and retold of their youthful fighting days.

But whatever the program, whether it be games or dancing primarily, it is opened and closed with simple yet beautiful ritual, ritual that lends dignity and importance to the council over and above an ordinary campfire. The best of these is given us by Seton.†

Thus there are two kinds of council fires, *Little Council* and *Grand Council*. Little Council consists primarily of the games, along with a minimum of ritual and certain routine discussions. It takes place often. Grand Council is primarily dancing, with performers in costume, with all the ritual. It happens only once a week.

But even though none of these activities is desired, a council ring is still essential in a camp for purposes of evening meetings around the fire.

WHAT THE COUNCIL RING IS NOT

These it is not:

1. It is not an amphitheater, but a *circle* of benches around a fire, no more on one side than another.

2. It is not a mere spot for a campfire—it is sacred, hallowed by tradition. There is no walking across it.

3. It is not movable—its benches are permanent and fixed.

4. It *is not a fire altar* with benches around it—the fire is *on the level of the ground*, unprotected by logs or stones around it.

5. It is not a big, open space. Bigness ruins it. Its inner diameter is twenty-four feet.

---

* The following are recommended for the beginner: Julia M. Buttree, *Rhythm of the Redman* (New York: A. S. Barnes & Co., 1930); also Ernest Thompson Seton, *The Book of Woodcraft* (Garden City: Garden City Publishing Co., 1921).

† See Ernest Thompson Seton, *The Birch Bark Roll of Woodcraft* (New York: Brieger Press, 1925).

Picking the Spot

The big, good thing for which to look is this: A beautiful spot, in the heart of the woods, closed in with the lushness of vegetation, teeming, literally reeking with the things that grow! There must be a perfectly level, smooth surface twenty-four feet in diameter, but beyond that, the prime concern is natural beauty. Often this beauty spot is high up, which may be well, but the beauty of trees and bushes is more to be desired than distant vistas, for the trees serve to wall it in, to shut out the confusing and distracting sights and sounds, to make the spoken word in the ring more audible. A solid bank of trees around it is ideal, trees tall enough to form a Gothic arch of green high overhead, more arrestingly beautiful from the light of the campfire below than any man-made cathedral, and through the leafy pattern of which may filter the sunlight by day and the moonlight by night. It must be close to the campsite, yet far enough away to escape the clatter and bang of work about the place, far enough from the lake to escape the pounding of waves and the distressing winds.

This we must remember: the ring is to be built for the programs that will take place there. And everything about the spot must be conducive to a well-presented and entirely audible program, well safeguarded from all that is distracting in the way of sight, sound, odor, and feeling.

Building the Ring

First make sure that the spot selected can be leveled to an even and smooth surface—if there are projecting roots or large imbedded rocks just beneath the surface the smoothness required for games and dancing cannot be achieved.

The width of the council ring is twenty-four feet. If less than that, it is too small for the activities; if more, it is too large for effective speaking. Some camps have two adjoining council rings, one for Little Council or games alone, and the other for Grand Council consisting primarily of dancing. In this case the Grand Council ring for dancing alone may be larger, let us say twenty-eight or twenty-nine feet across, this larger size providing a more adequate space for the dancers and lending to the spectators a perspective in viewing the dancing that is lost when too close to it. The average camp, however, will want one council ring, an all-purpose one for story-telling, games, ceremonies and dancing, and for this the diameter of twenty-four feet should apply. This matter of size is of prime importance: Row after row of seats may be placed around the inner circle, but this inner circle should be no more or less than the size specified. If made larger a little experience in it is sure to lead to a desire to change it, but once built, it is there to stay. Better take the recommendation of those with long experience and accept without question the twenty-four-foot diameter.

Select a large tree, if possible, as the focal point of the ring, in front of which the council rock is to be placed. This "rock" is the bench on which sit the chiefs who are running the council, the judges and other dignitaries, and in front of which most of the activities take place. There should be a space of three or four feet between the tree and the back of the council rock.

By means of a stake and a twelve-foot rope mark out the twenty-four-foot circle and drive stakes at intervals of every few feet around it.

Now we are ready to build the benches: And be it known that these benches are permanent and immovable, fixed securely to the ground. If they can be moved the campers are sure to move them to suit their own fancy, but if made stationary, the chief of the council knows before he arrives that all will be seated in proper positions.

First, let us assume that we are to make a simple ring of one row of benches, such as shown in the plan in Figure 195. There are several ways to construct the benches, depending on the natural setting and the facilities it offers—logs, half-logs, or planks. If two-inch planks are available, the easiest way is to cut them into five-foot lengths and nail them to sections of logs laid on the ground as supports, as shown in A, Figure 196. These supporting logs should be about twelve inches in diameter and fifteen inches long. They should be placed around the edge of the ring, radiating from the center, so spaced that the ends of two adjoining planks can be nailed to each as in A. The diagram indicates no backs to the benches, but to gain the end of having the campers comfortably seated and thoroughly at ease at all times, it is better that backs be provided. This is easily done by driving poles in the ground just behind the seats, giving them a slight backward lean, and nailing them to the logs on which the planks rest. If the poles are eighteen inches above the seat, the usual height of a chair back, and six-inch planks nailed to them at the top, a comfortable seat results.

Another common way to build the benches is to sink two six-inch poles in the ground every five feet around the circle as in B, Figure 196, allowing them to project upward twelve inches. To the tops of these the two-inch planks, five feet long, are nailed to form the circle.

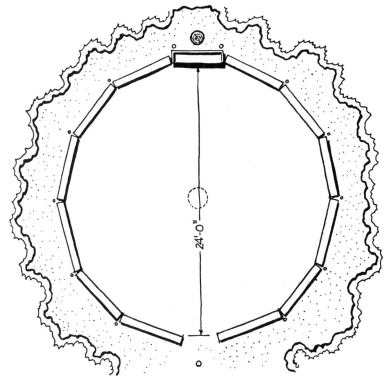

Figure 195. PLAN FOR A SMALL COUNCIL RING

This method makes a more permanent and substantial ring but takes a little longer to construct.

If planks are not to be had and logs are available in abundance, they may be split in half and used instead, elevated if need be on supporting cross-poles resting on the ground.

Note in Figure 195 that *there is only one entrance to the council ring,* this directly opposite the council rock. There seems to be a universal desire, on the part of those who are designing council rings, to build more entrances, but each opening constitutes a break in the circle that tends to destroy the unity of feeling. One entrance is sufficient and that should be small.

The *council rock* is a more elaborate bench, six feet long and eighteen inches high. In a simple council ring such as that shown in Figure 195 the mere fact that the council rock is made higher may be sufficient to set it off from the rest of the circle, although it is

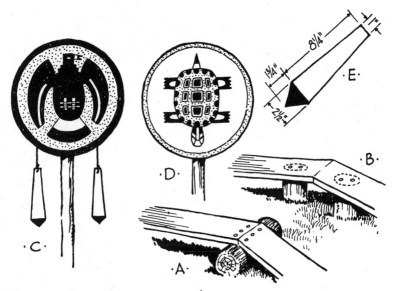

Figure 196. BENCHES, PLAQUES, AND WOODEN FEATHERS FOR THE COUNCIL RING

always desirable to build a more ornamental back for it, such as a fancy latticework of rustic poles.

About fifty people can be accommodated in a ring consisting of one row of benches as described. If more seats are needed the rear rows should be elevated enough so that the entire ring is visible to all when seated. In a ring consisting merely of two rows of benches, the front row may be made twelve inches high and the second row eighteen inches high, placed eighteen inches behind the first, but if more than two rows are to be built, one of two methods may be used: The seats may be built up from the level of the ground in bleacher fashion, or the ring may be excavated as shown in the sketch of the elaborate ring in Figure 197. The latter method is by all odds the better if the ground is dry enough and the drainage adequate to permit excavation. When so sunk an overflow crowd can be accommodated by having them stand around the outside circle, an arrangement that would be impossible if seats were elevated in bleacher fashion.

To make the excavated ring, remove the earth across the twenty-four-foot circle to a depth of twenty-four inches. Terrace the sides into two steps, each twelve inches high, as shown in Figure 197. This permits three rows of benches, the back row being on the level of the ground. Sink the posts as shown, allowing them to extend two inches above the ground, and nail on the two-inch planks, thus making the seats sixteen inches high. The entrance as usual is directly opposite the council rock. If much dancing is to take place in a ring of this type it is well to leave a very narrow passageway one foot wide either side of the council rock to serve as an entrance for the dancers. These passageways should not be stepped but rather should slope down gradually so that the dancers may dance in without danger of stumbling. If no more than one foot wide, these entrances will not detract from the impression of a completely enclosed circle, so essential in council-ring planning.

Should a still larger ring be needed, seats may be built in bleacher fashion behind the last row of benches, making each tier twelve inches higher than the one in front of it.

The remaining task is to build the *blanket rack* behind the council rock. For this two upright poles are erected at the back corners of the council rock, each five inches thick and eight feet high, across the top of which a pole is nailed parallel to the ground, as shown in the drawing of the section in Figure 197. Over the top of this framework a colorful Indian blanket should be hung, forming a background to the council rock and providing a picturesque drop in front of which the drama of the council proceeds. Without it the council ring, no matter how elaborately it may be constructed, seems to be wanting in some vital element.

The Adornment of the Council Ring

A simple ring of benches located in a beautiful spot in the woods may seem sufficiently appropriate without further adornment, but

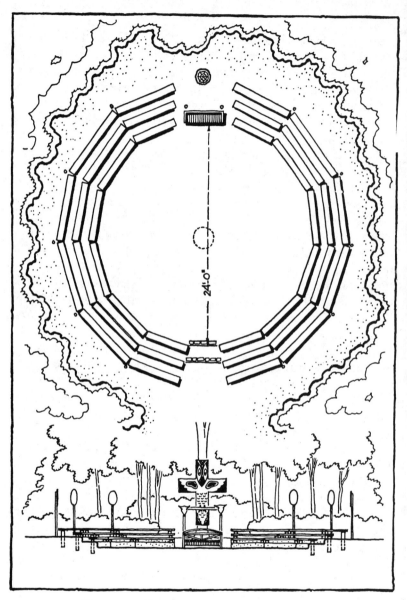

Figure 197. PLAN FOR A LARGE COUNCIL RING

since the very essence of the council ring is beauty, symbolism and imaginative appeal, and since it is Indian in origin and nature, it is always better to color it by drawing from the Indian's inexhaustible wealth of design.

There are several ways of accomplishing this:

Council-Rock Blanket.—We have already indicated the need for a blanket rack behind the council rock over which a colorful Indian blanket is hung. This blanket is removed after each council, of course, and becomes an ornament only when the council is in session. Many a camp makes its own council blanket by using a beautiful, draping cloth and painting or appliqueing the design on it.

Totem Poles.—Opposite the council rock and outside of the entrance is the place for the totem pole. Minus this, a council ring seems incomplete. In fact some council rings have three totem poles which, together with the thunderbird to be discussed presently, provide a totem decoration at each of the cardinal directions of the ring. All are placed outside the rows of benches. The making of the totem poles is described in Chapter XXIV.

Thunderbird.—The main object in placing the council rock four feet in front of a large tree if possible is to utilize the tree as a support for the thunderbird. These grotesque, bizarre birds, more than any other single factor, give to the council ring that unique, primitive quality without which it seems to be no more than an ordinary campfire circle.

The thunderbird may be as large as ten to twelve feet high with a wing spread equally large, hung high enough on the tree so that his feet are visible above the blanket behind the council rock. There he keeps constant and endless vigil over the council ring, day and night, whether or not the ring is in use. The design and construction of these birds are set forth in Chapter XXIV, "Totem Poles."

Totem Plaques.—One of the simplest yet most effective means of ornamentation for a council ring is the use of many round plaques on which totem symbols are painted, placed at intervals around the ring and nailed to the outer row of benches. Such plaques are shown at C and D in Figure 196. The easiest way to make these is to use ordinary large barrel tops nailed to saplings and erected, one behind each intersection of the planks in the outer row of benches—see the drawing of the section in Figure 197. The bottom of the plaque should be four feet above the rear bench. Ten of these plaques are required to complete the circle of the ring.

As to design, only authentic Indian symbols should be used, painted on in vivid colors. The wealth of Indian design in depicting animals, birds, and geometric patterns is so limitless that no one need want for appropriate plaque suggestions, but we must remember that the need is for *symbols*, never complete pictures. In this type of decoration it is always better to copy original Indian designs just as they are than to attempt to improve upon them—rather than resulting in improvement such effects are usually fatal. If each plaque is different, there is new imaginative appeal wherever one looks around the ring.

Symbolic Feathers.—Another interesting device for use in conjunction with the totem plaque is symbolic wooden eagle feathers hung beneath the plaques. These are made of quarter-inch strips, shaped as in E, Figure 196, measuring ten inches long and two-and-one-half inches wide at the widest point. In imitation of eagle feathers, these are painted white with black tips at the bottom as shown. They should be suspended with *string* and not wire, one on each side of the plaque, as shown in C, Figure 196, so that they will freely twirl and move in the wind. This movement of the feathers is one of the most intriguing features about them—they swing back and forth with a walking motion, one in one direction and the other in another, they twirl and spin, and in general attract the attention of the spectators not only to them but to the plaque to which they are suspended. The use of string to hang them necessitates frequent rehanging, but it makes possible the essential movement that wire precludes.

Buffalo Skulls.—Everyone familiar with the Plains Indians will realize the importance of the buffalo skull in his philosophy of life and the appropriateness of a wooden imitation of it as a council-ring adornment. In the old days each lodge possessed its buffalo skull in honor of this generous animal, looked upon as the giver and sustainer of life. Its horns were the badge of leadership. It symbolized long life and plenty. It was a gentle totem, referred to with lovable names.

Two wooden buffalo skulls are appropriate indeed, one placed on each of the top corners of the blanket rack behind the council rock. And a third may well be placed on the ground in front of the drums before the council rock. The making of these skulls from wood is set forth in Chapter XXIV, "Totem Poles."

Tepees.—As a background to the council ring, tepees are the proper thing. One or two of these placed behind and to one side of the council rock not only seem to belong to the setting but are useful as property lodges where the materials used in council are kept. The making of the tepees is described in Chapter II of Part I, "Tepees of the Plains."

INDOOR COUNCIL RINGS

Not always can we use the outdoor council ring, for the weather is sometimes rainy and cold, the ground wet—and we are forced indoors. Then, if ever, the tonic of a joyous evening is needed to warm the dampened spirits, and so an indoor council arrangement of some sort is important.

It was in an inclosed council ring that the Indians of the North met this need, a circular or octagonal building often referred to as the roundhouse, just large enough to accommodate the circle of benches, with low side walls from which the roof sloped upwards to a point in the middle. These are still many in number in the Indian country, even though a little dilapidated, reminiscent of a glory that used to be, yet still vibrant with atmosphere. We need but to sit in one when the dances are on to be convinced that these circular walls so close behind the benches, better than any other arrangement, retain and conserve that atmosphere so precious to council, so difficult to conjure up, and so easily lost, so easily evaporated into thin air if there is too much open space around the circle.

In camps today such an inclosed council ring would be ideal but as a rule we use instead the camp recreation building or dining hall. With proper handling a council can be there set up that will leave little to be desired.

The conditions as to size are the same as outdoors—an open circle twenty-four feet in diameter. The benches must, of course, be movable since the hall will be used for many purposes, but in order to eliminate the necessity of laying out a twenty-four-foot circle preliminary to each council, a circle of this size should be painted on the floor, around which the benches can be quickly placed. One camp of which I know has not only painted such a circle on the floor but has covered the entire area of the twenty-four-foot ring with a reproduction of a Navajo sand painting, applied with enamel in vivid colors. The atmosphere lent by these painted symbols is indescribable, but whether or not a camp should find this practical, the circular line marking out the ring should always be possible without damaging the floor for other uses.

As in the outdoor ring, a council rock is needed and for this a settee or large bench may be used. And behind it should be the rack for the blanket, a movable framework of cedar poles which can be shoved up behind the council rock at the beginning of the ·council and pushed aside afterwards.

Set up in this way and aided by the use of all the appropriate adornment and symbolism that may be available, we have a setting in which the true atmosphere of council can be conjured up so as to cause the campers to forget that, after all, they are sitting in a modern building of prosaic type.

INDEX

187

74 75 76 77 10 9 8 7 6 5 4 3 2 1